Black Country Chronicles

The proceeds from the sales of this book will be donated to

The County Air Ambulance, Birmingham, B23 6QP
and
The Down's Syndrome Association, Teddington, TW11 9PS

BLACK COUNTRY CHRONICLES

TOM LARKIN

The History Press

First published in 2009 by
The History Press
The Mill · Brimscombe Port ·
Stroud · Gloucestershire · GL5 2QG
www.thehistorypress.co.uk

British Library Cataloguing in Publication Data
A catalogue record for this book is available from the British Library.

ISBN 978-0-7509-5084-8

Typeset in 10.5/13pt Sabon
Typesetting and origination by
The History Press.

Contents

Acknowledgements

I am indebted to the many people who have contributed to this book but who wish to remain anonymous; sadly some of them are no longer with us, however, they all wanted their stories to be told so that future generations could learn from them. They asked that any proceeds should be donated to local charities.

I would like to thank members of the Black Country Memories Club for their assistance, because for a long time they have done so much to keep the region's proud traditions and history alive.

In addition, thanks are due to William Howe, Alan Tranter. Mrs E. Chattin, Megan Fitzgerald Plummer, Gerald Hanrahan, Bill Hasketh, George Henry Davies, C.T. Callaghan, Linda Lawton, Bill Comer and Reg Aston for providing photographs that give a vivid visual portrait of the area during the twentieth century.

Also, I want to acknowledge the crucial help received from members of the Lunt Tenants and Residents Association, particularly Ann Ramsbottom, Jean Hasketh and Ann Nightingale, without whom the entire project would have been impossible. Thanks are also due to Michael James Ealey for his financial support.

Finally, I would like to thank my wife, Emily, for her patience and encouragement over many years and also Professor Carl Chinn, not only for his general advice but also for kindly contributing such a generous foreword.

This book is dedicated to all of you.

Tom Larkin

Foreword

by Professor Carl Chinn MBE

B*lack Country Chronicles* is not a dry recording of events set down in a chronological order; rather it is a fascinating and multi-faceted narrative of twentieth-century life in the Black Country that draws in the reader and encourages more research. Tom Larkin and the other members of the Black Country Memories Club have long been determined that the way of life, sacrifices, hardships and day-to-day living of themselves, their moms and dads, and their forebears should not be allowed to sink into the oblivion of history; instead they should be passed on as part of the past that is remembered and handed on to those yet to come. This book achieves their aim.

Importantly, it embeds the history of Black Country firmly within the twentieth-century history of Britain. This careful attention to the contexts of time and place ensures that the Black Country is not regarded as some quaint region on the margins of British society, but that it is recognised as a significant place whose people made major contributions to the economic well-being of their country, even though many of them suffered grievously – along with others elsewhere – because of the ravages of the Depression of the 1920s and 1930s.

Throughout this work and via his considered compilation, Tom Larkin is at pains to avoid a mawkish sentimentality when writing about working-class life. He neither romanticises nor exaggerates, but seeks to bring to the fore the harsh conditions, bad housing, polluted environment, low standards of hygiene and tough discipline that dominated people's lives. Paying due regard to the General Strike of 1926 and the political situation, Tom examines how people struggled to cope with unemployment and poverty. He also emphasises the significance of work and of the Black Country philosophy of 'if yow dow work, yow dow ate', as well as the harsh employment rules which governed working lives.

But this is more than a tale of hardships; it is a story of sights and sounds, street vendors, high days and holidays, fashions, religious beliefs, dance halls, wireless-listening, Christmas celebrations, and community lynchpins like corner shops. Based on the memories of the members of the Black Country Memories Club and on documents from the time, this is a compelling work that emphasises human resilience and especially that of working folk. They provide a sharp contrast to the indifference shown by the men (and it was mostly men) in positions of power and influence.

Professor Carl Chinn MBE

Introduction

The following pages are part of a comprehensive compilation of personal reminiscences and eyewitness accounts contributed by senior citizens from all walks of life, which attempt to give an insight into the lives of ordinary Black Country people from the beginning of the twentieth century onwards.

These memories cover important events that illustrate the quality of life experienced by our grandparents and parents, a lifestyle that has now vanished.

From these comments it is quite evident that older people have become very concerned that their heritage, history and culture is being diminished with the passing of time. They accept that things cannot remain the same forever, and that there is a need to move on, but they feel strongly that the sacrifices made by previous generations need to be recorded before they become totally forgotten.

They also believe it is equally important to record other facets of daily life appertaining to such matters as entertainment, sport, religion, courting and marriage, discipline in the home, food, politics and overall standards of public behaviour.

At the turn of the twentieth century, the Black Country region was looked upon as an area of ugly landscapes, unclean waterways and smoking chimneystacks permanently polluting the atmosphere and creating a grim environment. Without doubt there are numerous collections of photographic material that give a limited visual impression of the past; these are mainly concerned with buildings, artefacts and souvenirs. There is a great shortage of details and facts documenting how our forebears coped with all the hardships they experienced on a daily basis.

What little written information there is available tends to be a mixture of mawkish sentimentality, that gives a misleading impression that life in the old communities had a lot to commend it and that in many ways society in the 1920s, '30s, '40s and '50s was more caring and civilised than it is today.

Many of the harsh realities, sacrifices and momentous achievements of our forebears will be highlighted along with some of the humorous moments shared among family and friends. Children could play safely in the streets or in open fields from dawn to dusk without fear, doors to houses could be left open for everyone to come and go as they pleased. This book is also about friends, neighbours, families and social values.

If future generations are to learn the true facts of how their grandparents and parents dealt with the pressures and challenges of two world wars, mass unemployment, economic depression, widespread poverty and squalor; it becomes even more obvious why the relevant details need to be documented. Hopefully, these observations will encourage the younger generation to find out more about their own family and the contribution they made to the Black Country's proud reputation as the 'Workshop of the World'.

Every era produces problems affecting the quality of life that differs from previous periods of history. In the main, people's lifestyles are determined by the type of governments they encounter over a certain time span and, above all, the various policies these individual administrations chose to implement. By looking back at those policies which shaped people's lives from the beginning of the twentieth century, it is possible to portray a society totally different from the one we live in today.

In 1900 the Labour Party was officially established and following the death of Queen Victoria in 1901, a marked period of transition and innovation began with the succession of Edward VII heralding a totally new era.

At the start of the new century the Boer War was still in progress and would not be resolved until 1902 and before long, unskilled workers in particular started to press for improved wages and better working conditions. Up until then most existing unions were very small in membership, but this situation rapidly changed, individual sections began to amalgamate to give themselves greater bargaining power and soon after, numerous scattered strikes took place in engineering, mining, heavy manufacturing industries and on the railways.

Initially during the opening years of the century there was a slight improvement in overall social conditions – for instance the introduction of compulsory school medical inspections in 1907 – and in that same year the first ever old-age pensions were introduced (albeit restricted to people over seventy).

This amounted to 5*s* for a single pensioner and 7*s* 6*d* for a married couple. Then, in 1909, the first official labour exchange was established and soon one appeared in every city and town. Finally, in 1911, the eagerly-awaited Shops Act was passed giving all shop employees the absolute right to a half-day holiday a week.

This was a period when the region was accepted as the undisputed manufacturing powerhouse of the nation. However, alongside all this industrial prosperity there existed great extremes of wealth for a selected few but for the majority of working-class families there were large areas of widespread poverty and squalor.

For most of the workforce the normal week consisted of toiling in heavy industries and foundries in the most appalling working conditions for long hours, in return for a pittance of a wage. Many walked to their place of employment, a distance varying from anything between 1 or 2 miles, whatever the weather, because they simply couldn't afford the bus fare.

After enduring years of that type of hard graft and unhealthy working environment, it was little wonder that so many men and women became physically worn out in their early fifties. It was a time when even the very idea of an annual two weeks' holiday with pay was still many years away.

With such low wages, thousands of households survived on a basic diet of meat scraps, stew, potatoes, rabbit and all manner of cheap sub-standard food. Children from large families would regularly be restricted to nothing more than dripping on bread sandwiches or the occasional rare treat of jam.

In reality, the only form of help for those living on the breadline was that provided by local church or chapel organisations and other similar voluntary groups; other than that they relied on the charity of relatives or caring neighbours.

Throughout this time, successive governments were strongly opposed to any suggestions of providing a national welfare safety net, and this explains why work became the dominant issue in people's lives. Most senior citizens, when discussing the past, constantly remark that in those days, becoming unemployed was a disaster to avoid at all costs. As a result it was common practice for the man of the house to go to work and shrug off any sickness he may have developed. They faced this dilemma no matter how ill they felt, because they could not risk being suspended or sacked, with so many unemployed people seeking any type of job.

It was also an era when the status of women was clearly defined with motherhood being regarded as their vocation in life. This often meant struggling to make ends meet and running a home on a ridiculously inadequate weekly allowance by continually scrimping and making-do.

All of these social problems were temporarily put on hold when war broke out in 1914 and subsequently, among many other occurences, led to drastic changes in outdated attitudes towards the accepted role of women in society. This was because wartime circumstances forced the government to recruit them for vital war work and to fill vacancies created by more and more men being conscripted.

Understandably people make comparisons about the world they grew up in and the present day; in doing so a minority often conclude that 'things were much better in the old days'. Realistically, much of that type of thinking is based on sheer misty-eyed nostalgia.

It is a simplistic observation that overlooks the squalid living standards and deplorable poverty that was once so commonplace. What is undoubtedly true, is the claim made that those who lived through those decades were unique in so many ways.

The evidence justifying that description of our parents and grandparents shows that in spite of endless betrayals by successive governments, they overcame the challenges they faced and went on to establish massive social changes and the improved quality of life that today's generation of youngsters now benefit from.

Many older people feel that this huge achievement of establishing the welfare state, National Health Service, higher living standards, better education and higher pensions has never been fully acknowledged by modern historians.

This becomes evident from reading accounts of the early decades of the Black Country's twentieth-century history, which tends to skate over the appalling postwar poverty and unemployment that took place after the end of the First World War, as well as the broken promises made by politicians to provide a better life. Far from that happening when the war ended in 1918, after a brief period of prosperity, serious and widespread unemployment returned on an even larger scale.

It was to be the beginning of two decades of economic slump, poverty and wage cuts that would culminate in the 1926 general strike, and '30s depression.

CHAPTER ONE

The Impact of the First World War

From the beginning, the First World War was greeted with great enthusiasm by young men in the Black Country, who rushed in large numbers to answer the patriotic call to arms displayed on government posters proclaiming Kitchener's emotional recruiting message 'YOUR COUNTRY NEEDS YOU'. So many young men volunteered well before real conscription was introduced in 1916 for all young men from the age of eighteen, for a mixture of reasons.

Judging from comments made by those who recall this patriotic response, the keenness to volunteer involved sheer youthful excitement, love of country, belief in a cause worth fighting for, an opportunity for escaping from persistent unemployment, plus a chance to see a little of the world. Whichever of those factors motivated them, it revealed a lot about the type of society that existed at the time. Few of those volunteers would have anticipated that after the four years of carnage, their lives would be shaped and changed in a way no one could have imagined.

This became evident following the horror and slaughter resulting from countless battles over mud-covered ground just to gain a pointless few yards of territory at a cost of thousands of lives. Those who did return from this hell on earth found it difficult to talk about their dreadful experiences, choosing to maintain an understandable silence concerning

Some Black Country soldiers of the First World War.

incidents they had witnessed. Some developed a grim determination to campaign for and demand a better life and fairer society, a minority even believed government promises of building a future 'land fit for heroes', until it became clear that this was simply standard political claptrap.

Less than three years after hostilities ceased, unemployment figures in the Black Country included over a third of returning ex-servicemen.

With the fall in the price of manufacturing goods during this early post-war period, many local firms introduced a severe policy of cut-backs in operating costs, which created serious unemployment, and thousands of households began to experience a lower weekly living standard, worse than they had had in the pre-war years. This grim period reflects the harsh realities of post-war Black Country life endured by those who had returned from the nightmare of trench warfare. For those, in particular, daily civilian life became extremely difficult to adjust to.

Factual accounts of what daily conditions were really like portray an appalling scenario of events with people's recollections of regularly seeing groups of unemployed ex-servicemen standing on street corners, or watching the walking wounded balancing on crutches while they attempted to sell boxes of matches to passers by. Even worse was the sight of men having to resort to begging for a few pennies to feed their families.

Thousands merely existed from week to week, and not surprisingly they became more and more bitter over the failure of politicians from all parties to find some type of solution to ease their plight.

It was common knowledge that prior to the war lots of factories had continued to use totally out-dated machinery. As a result, industries in areas such as the Black Country were completely exposed to the post-war challenge of foreign competition leading to the crisis of widespread unemployment, and those same politicians had done nothing to encourage investment in new machinery and modern technology.

Women's contribution to the First World War

In 1903, Emmeline Pankhurst had founded the Women's Social and Political Union, known later as the Suffragette movement, that campaigned for equal rights for women and the right to vote. The demands of modern warfare resulted in the direct involvement of more and more women during the First World War. When hostilities finally ended, public opinion regarding the role of women in society changed dramatically.

No longer was it perceived that a woman was destined to play the part of the dutiful, obedient housewife, relying solely on the husband for financial stability; certainly not after thousands of married women had undertaken work and responsibilities that had previously been regarded as strictly for men.

They had been recruited and trained by the government to take on all types of duties to maintain vital public services, such as working on the railways, driving buses, delivering mail and, most crucial of all, working in factories to boost essential war output, mainly making shells and munitions.

From 1915 much of this shift work producing ammunition and shells was done in what was a highly dangerous working environment with all the unavoidable unhealthy cordite and chemical ingredients required to produce these vital weapons of war. At times their skin would take on a yellowish tint, which was so obvious it led to them being referred to as 'canaries', so much so that a special medal was introduced, and awarded to local Black Country women engaged on this hazardous work in recognition of 'their courageous contribution to the war effort'.

Then in 1917, various branches of the armed services were established together with numerous medical units, which many women chose to join as an alternative option to factory work. Inevitably when peace arrived there began a real sustained movement to improve the status of women in society. This included entry into universities and the right to obtain positions in the civil service previously closed to them, as well as the opportunity to join trade unions.

An early success was achieved in 1918, when the government agreed to allow the vote for all women over 30, no doubt in recognition of their contribution to the war effort; but for both men and women, the early postwar years were to become a depressing period of economic instability leading to a great deal of industrial unrest and change.

This led to a national rail strike in 1919, and by 1921 unemployment had continued to escalate at an alarming rate. In turn, the quality of life deteriorated to almost desperation levels for many families.

This happened just as the first permanent war memorials started to appear in towns and villages all over the region, and at the same time, the rapid rise in the numbers of jobless ex-servicemen became a stark reminder of false political promises.

By 1923, out of sheer desperation, many local ex-servicemen began to travel as far as London and other large cities, looking for some kind of regular work. A minority even took the more drastic step of emigrating to other countries such as South Africa, Canada, Australia and New Zealand to escape and hopefully ensure a better quality of life for themselves, and more importantly, their children.

They were wise to take such dramatic steps, because throughout the remainder of the 1920s, and the even more severe early 1930s, unemployment, low wages, serious poverty, and appalling working and living conditions would continue to be part of everyday life.

CHAPTER TWO

Industry and the Community

Only those who actually experienced, at first hand, the far-reaching impact of industries on Black Country society can possibly describe their overall influence on thousands of households. It was not simply the fact that they virtually guaranteed regular employment, but the numerous ways they became involved in so many facets of community activities.

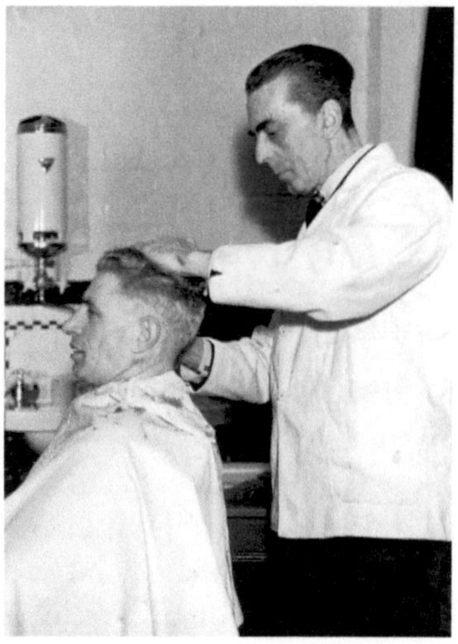

Villier's Works barber in Wolverhampton.

This explains why their decline had social implications on top of the obvious economic consequences. It is sometimes forgotten, for example, that many large business enterprises adopted a policy of building houses specifically for their local workforce. They also provided first-class recreational facilities which employees could enjoy at little cost; they built social clubs, promoted drama groups, encouraged all types of hobbies, organised regular dances, works outings, Christmas parties and the inevitable annual employees' works dinner and dance. A few large firms even had their own barbers on the premises for the benefit of the workers. Most firms also regularly assisted in community projects, by making a substantial financial contribution.

Their impact on local family day-to-day life was considerable. It was customary for a father, son, and often daughter to work for the same company, and upon leaving school, the youngest member of a

GKN Sports Pavilion, Hall Street, Darlaston.

household would become an apprentice; all of this established a loyal family commitment to the prosperity and future well-being of the particular firm that employed them. Most people recall how in the old days it was commonplace for whole families to devote their total working life to one company, clocking up long years of service. They were openly proud that the products they helped to make were admired the world over, and fathers believed strongly in the value of an apprenticeship that gave their children an opportunity to learn a worthwhile trade which secured their future.

Cutbacks in wages and the General Strike of 1926

By 1923/4, the economic postwar slump and widening social problems convinced the government that certain harsh choices had to be taken regarding national expenditure. Subsequently, recommendations were made on steps that needed to be taken regarding cutbacks. It was decided to drastically scale down practically all public services, extend the hours worked in a normal week and most controversial of all, reduce wages. Not surprisingly, this packet of unpopular measures quickly fanned the flames of deep simmering unrest.

Around the time when the government's proposals were being published, various initiatives had been launched throughout the Black Country. They included efforts to persuade local councils to commence much-needed public works schemes as a direct means of easing unemployment.

Up to 1925, many working-class families just about managed to survive from week to week, and when things got really bad, neighbours and relatives would do what they could to help the less fortunate in their hour of need.

Predictably in 1926, the deteriorating economic crisis led to the first ever national strike, when the Trade Union Congress (TUC) decided to back the miners in their outright opposition to wage cuts, and longer working hours. A significant factor which influenced the Black Country workforce to back direct action, was that unemployment had come close to, or actually reached 25 per cent among the potential male workforce in Walsall, Dudley, West Bromwich and Wolverhampton. This provided an added incentive and determination to support the mining unions.

According to elderly residents living in the region at that time, it soon became obvious that very little thought had been given to the actual organisation of the strike apart from Central Emergency Committees, operating in every town, each one made up of a representative from every trade union branch.

Throughout the conflict newspaper publication was suspended, other than the central government sponsored *British Gazette*, while locally the *Express & Star* attempted to keep people informed about day-to-day developments by producing a penny news sheet. The government recruited volunteers to act as special constables, and to drive buses, charabancs (coaches), and delivery trucks with the idea of driving them through picket lines if necessary.

All bus and passenger train services ground to a halt. Essential food supplies were switched to the road, and within a short space of time this inevitably brought about ugly clashes, involving strikers and those who were totally against the aims of the strike.

It resulted in confrontations such as the one at Cleveland Road bus depot in Wolverhampton, during which dedicated strike breakers attempted to drive a bus away. After a series of minor scuffles with pickets, they reluctantly accepted defeat.

Over in Walsall, a similar incident took place when a private charabanc firm tried to run a passenger service from outside the old courthouse to Birmingham, which also ended in failure when an angry crowd gathered preventing it leaving and throughout the dispute troops were used to move supplies from the docks, and also to protect essential power stations.

The collapse of the General Strike

In every town, prominent politicians and union officials were addressing meetings while the government responded by encouraging religious leaders to speak out against what it called potential public anarchy. One of its leading figures, Winston Churchill, went further by suggesting the dispute was a revolutionary threat.

Regular BBC wireless bulletins were transmitted giving up to date news of the state of affairs, but the contents were inevitably government-slanted because they had taken control of all broadcasting. In Walsall, committees were established to supervise distribution of food, and other essential items, as more and more militant strikers moved to block vehicles driving away from railway stations, and supply depots.

At Bilston Central station, tempers flared when groups of pickets became directly involved with policemen attempting to clear a safe passage for delivery vehicles. Ultimately, numerous claims of over-zealous use of force was levelled at the police, which temporarily soured what had been fairly good-humoured relations between the law and strikers.

The social consequences soon began to emerge with desperate families from Darlaston and Willenhall descending on Bentley Common to go coal-picking, utilising every type of household implement at their disposal, be it pick-axe, shovel, trowel, bucket or spade in the process. For almost every household this

Ramsay MacDonald addressing a crowd in Wolverhampton in the 1920s. (Reproduced by permission of the Express & Star, *Wolverhampton)*

was the only means of ensuring the crucial domestic fire they needed for heating and cooking was maintained, because as the strike continued, money to purchase essential household fuel soon dried up.

To transport the precious pieces of salvaged coal they used old prams, wheelbarrows or some would build wooden pushcarts made out of scrounged boxes. This practice of digging on abandoned coal sites would, less than a decade later, be repeated on a much larger scale during the disastrous depression.

In the Leamore and Bloxwich areas of Walsall mobile kitchens began to appear to provide for those families in most desperate need. The overall situation was made much worse for a minority not entitled to certain benefit payments and consequently they were forced to rely on Poor Law relief.

The vast majority of strikers were further angered by the refusal of Ramsay MacDonald, the then leader of the Labour Party, to publicly endorse the aims of the strike. This decision would later on have much wider repercussions both for him and his party.

At the beginning of the strike, its aims had been clear but suddenly on 12 May 1926 it all came to a bitter controversial end, mainly because less militant members of the TUC had become concerned about a legal challenge suggesting that certain aspects could be shown to be illegal under existing laws. Also, doubts began to surface regarding sufficient funds being available to cover strike pay for everyone involved.

This unexpected turnabout resulted in months of bitterness and claims of a sell-out, followed by even greater anger when it became known that a proportion of those on strike would not be offered their jobs back by some employers.

Consequently, the only nationwide General Strike in the Britain's history collapsed in total confusion and failure, with no improvements secured in weekly wages and no reduction in the length of the normal working week, which were the two main aims of the conflict.

CHAPTER THREE

The Depression Begins

The fiasco of the General Strike was merely the beginning of a whole chapter of disastrous events, which would create extremes of hardship lasting for most of the 1930s. People had hardly recovered from the traumas of the First World War, and the General Strike before being confronted by an economic disaster brought about the collapse of the all-powerful American stock market. This occurred on Wall Street in October 1929, and overnight set in motion a devastating industrial collapse, which swept through a western world heavily dependent on a thriving American economy. By August 1930, unemployment in Britain rose above the 2 million mark.

In heavily industrialised regions such as the Black Country, it quickly brought about the worst Depression ever known with massive unemployment, privation and in 1931 the introduction of the evil 'means test' system, resulting in widespread social despair for many families.

Only those who lived through that unforgettable period can thoroughly describe the unimaginable suffering. Many retain bitter memories of the vicious cuts in dole pay, which forced housewives to purchase food on the 'weekly slate' at local corner shops. This was the only way that they could put a meagre meal on the table, other than by humiliating themselves by pledging their few possessions at the nearest pawn shop to make ends meet.

Once-proud men and women had to swallow their pride, and appear before local 'Public Assistance Boards', to plead for extra help to feed their families. There are numerous first-hand accounts of homes being subjected to the despised means test, often involving a visit from officials, with the authority to thoroughly investigate a family's most intimate, and private financial circumstances.

Every aspect of a family's lifestyle was probed, even down to the small amount earned by any of the children doing a paper round, or helping out in a local shop. Most controversial of all was the legal right given to these bureaucrats to confiscate items of furniture in a home, which in their judgement amounted to an unnecessary luxury. Such possessions were not allowed under means test regulations and were therefore placed in a public auction for general sale; even then the unfortunate family could still find their level of weekly state subsistence reduced without any right of appeal.

Not surprisingly, this type of personal intrusion into people's lives simply inflamed already bitter feelings, which explains why there are still unhappy memories of these occurrences, ensuring a lasting contempt and suspicion of all types of officialdom that has survived into the present day.

Desperate measures

More than twenty years on from the government's commitment to create a better quality of life for returning servicemen, it was clear that this promised utopia was as far away as ever. The outcome of the General Election in June 1929 saw Ramsay MacDonald become Prime Minister of a minority administration, which immediately found it necessary to recommend sweeping cuts in public expenditure to parliament to deal with the increasing economic slump. These draconian proposals included a reduction of 5 per cent to 15 per cent in the wages of public employees and also weekly dole payments

Food, at that particular time, was relatively cheap, but few families were able to benefit from that situation because they were unable to purchase with ready cash. It was certainly never an option for the thousands struggling to make ends meet on inadequate dole money or terribly low weekly wages. Most housewives shopped on a daily basis for all perishable items of food, because many small slum properties either possessed severely restricted food storage facilities, or none at all.

In the middle of the week, many women relied on the good will of local shopkeepers who allowed them to make purchases on credit until Friday pay day. People who lived through those traumatic years never claim to have experienced symptoms of actual starvation, but a large number recollect as a child being sent to bed still feeling very hungry.

Apart from the embarrassment of needing to purchase items 'on tick', the shortage of money also meant having to buy food that had started to go off and could therefore be obtained cheaply. Every corner shop operated this method of disposing of deteriorating food, especially in the hot summer months. Mostly it consisted of all kinds of bruised fruit, cooked meats, fly-blown meat, rotting potatoes, any type of stale confectionery and, of course, out of date cheese.

For those families at the rock bottom of the social scale, there was always the added indignity of having to buy individual cut slices of bread, corned meat and cheese – yet another lucrative system that enabled shopkeepers to make a handsome profit. With no form of social safety net, welfare benefits, child allowances or rent rebates,.such occurrences were commonplace throughout those stark years.

The deepening crisis brings an end to the minority Labour government

Early in 1931 a proposed target of severe cutbacks in public expenditure began to divide the government. Even so, Prime Minister Ramsay MacDonald somehow managed to obtain cabinet approval to proceed with them, albeit with only a slim two-vote majority. This created a situation that made it virtually impossible for his already shaky administration to continue in government, leaving him with no other option but to consult with the king, and after doing so, making a public statement to the effect 'that in the overall interests of the country, a temporary coalition administration would be formed made up of members from all three main political parties.'

To ensure continuity, he also revealed that an agreement had been reached that he should continue as Prime Minister, and a direct appeal was made to the whole nation asking for their vital support in order to bring about an urgent halt to the widening economic decline. It all resulted in serious implications for the Black Country and within a matter of months statistics for the area confirmed the grim facts that two-thirds of the workforce had become part of the ever-increasing list of long-term unemployed.

In every town in the Black Country, those statistics became more and more visibly evident with tragic scenes of desperate men returning home after spending yet another fruitless morning traipsing from one factory gate to another in the hope of finding work of any description. Recollections are still vivid for older residents of witnessing groups of disillusioned unemployed men wandering over the nearest fields where they would try and find a little temporary relief from their daily boredom by indulging in a game of 'pitch and toss' – yet another sombre reminder of those soul-destroying times. This traditional game involved drawing a thin line in the ground using the heel of the shoe, and then each player would take his turn at pitching a penny coin to try and place it as near as possible to it. The one who was closest was then entitled to pocket all the other coins that had fallen short.

Throughout the whole process youngsters would hang around, hoping to be offered the chance of acting as 'lookout' by perching themselves on top of a nearby bank to watch for any sign of a policeman, because all forms of public gambling were illegal. An early warning system was essential. There was never any shortage of volunteers willing to earn a few pennies reward for carrying out the task.

Towards the autumn of 1931, in spite of all the cuts in dole payments and public services, unemployment increased even further. This brought about bitter criticism of the coalition, and public disapproval of Ramsay MacDonald, its appointed leader.

CHAPTER FOUR

An All-Party Government

In September 1931, Ramsay MacDonald was predictably expelled from the Labour Party, but as Prime Minister of the temporary coalition government, he responded by calling a General Election. Throughout the ensuing bitter campaign he pleaded for people to vote solidly for those candidates standing under an all-party banner, as the only logical way of producing a strong, united government.

Although the electorate held grave doubts about the whole principal of coalition, they decided to give him another chance. Consequently a National Government was duly elected, consisting of members from all three main parties with a huge overall working majority.

This meant Ramsay MacDonald became head of a government, committed to a tough policy of taking harsh decisions to solve the nation's increasing economic problems. It included the establishment of local Public Assistance Committees, with responsibilities for administering the unforgettable means test.

The recurring problem of large-scale unemployment was to bring about decades of social deprivation, yet surprisingly, there is very little recorded facts that accurately illustrates the utter distress it created. The most familiar symbol of that shameful period of social history is usually confined to flickering newsreel pictures of the 1936 Jarrow to London march, involving 200 redundant shipyard workers. The fading pictures manage to depict their grim-faced determination to take their protest to the very centre of government.

There are even fewer details available of the subsequent response of the local Unemployment Assistance Board back in Jarrow to cut their dole money entitlement; the excuse being that while taking part in the march, they had made themselves unavailable for work in their hometown.

That march is still regarded as the most emotional image of the despair created by widespread unemployment, but people remember that all over the Black Country various forms of protests were taking place to highlight the plight of thousands of deprived families.

In Walsall, a group representing all types of tradesmen decided to set up a Volunteer Legion. They were prepared to carry out a variety of useful tasks that would be of benefit to their communities, and would at the same time help the unemployed to temporarily forget their feelings of frustration at government failure to provide them with full-time jobs.

The reaction to all this by the powers that be in Walsall was typically bureaucratic and short-sighted. They promptly rejected this enterprising proposal out of hand on the flimsy grounds that it might create a dangerous precedent, likely to threaten existing job demarcation rules.

Such historic events are part of the region's historic past, and many who lived through those trying times rightly complain that not enough is taught in today's schools about those appalling times.

Public reaction to the Depression

A sobering reminder of living conditions during the early 1930s was given considerable prominence in the columns of a local newspaper in 1931, with observations made by the vicar of All Saints' Church, Darlaston, who remarked 'unemployment is a tragic fact of life today and I have great sympathy for members of the parish who are out of work. I am certain there is a solution if only employers, politicians and workers lay aside all their prejudices.'

Typical 1930s back-to-back slum housing.

Hobbins Street, Wednesbury – a typical rear of Black Country back-to-back housing. (Reproduced by permission of Sandwell Community History and Archive Service)

Such outspoken thoughts from a prominent religious figure was surprising because it was a very rare and controversial thing in those days, but during that same week a similar message of despair emerged which also attracted wide publicity. These comments originated from a group of teachers based in Willenhall, Bilston and Darlaston, who regularly co-operated in organising events to raise money for The Poor Children's Fund. They had also decided that it was high time the public were made aware of the problem of childhood destitution. They underlined their annual appeal with a carefully worded joint statement declaring that they were 'becoming greatly disturbed by the growing number of schoolchildren from the three towns, who regularly tramped to school through bitter weather, clad in so-called shoes that are an apology for normal wintertime footwear.'

Hardly anyone would have been shocked at reading such revelations because most people frequently witnessed these circumstances themselves, and many would no doubt have expressed their disappointment that other symptoms of grinding poverty within their communities had not been highlighted at the same time.

Elderly citizens maintain even today, that the true level of poverty and suffering experienced by thousands of Black Country children who grew up in the 1930s has never been fully documented. Only actual eyewitnesses can fully portray how poverty created widespread malnutrition, which led to many children suffering from rickets, resulting solely from the lack of vital Vitamin D. It is impossible to ever forget the shameful sight of young children with bow legs and softening bones caused by the crippling disease, walking with iron supports attached to their legs.

Many of these unfortunate youngsters also endured the added hardship of living in back-to-back slum properties. A clear indication of the true depth of poverty came with the release of a survey, which confirmed that 40 per cent of local working-class children were daily existing on or just above the recognised poverty line.

Such appalling circumstances were never more evident than in the months leading up to Christmas, when throughout those weeks, the local *Express & Star*, through its popular columnist 'Quastor' ran a charity called The Poor Children's Christmas Fund from its Wolverhampton Office.

There are still people around who benefited from this enterprising initiative, which functioned on the simple formula of asking local traders to adopt a deprived family for Christmas day by donating 10*s* for food and small presents. Households throughout the region where invited to write in and apply for consideration as suitable beneficiaries. Every applicant was carefully vetted before being accepted and over the years the fund became an enormous success.

In 1935, the newspaper disclosed that a family of six under existing regulations received the princely weekly sum of £1 19*s* 6*d* unemployment benefit, which dramatically highlighted the desperate need for such a scheme to assist the less fortunate.

Widespread poverty instigates a campaign for a better quality of life

During this period, the savage economic crisis and the desperate scramble to find any type of employment would often mean taking a monotonous dead-end job with long hours and low wages. It would usually entail working in an unhealthy environment and primitive safety conditions. Obtaining employment became a priority and with no welfare state system there was no opportunity to be choosy, particularly knowing that every morning there would be others waiting outside the factory gates even more desperate to fill any vacancy, whatever the poor working circumstances.

Many believe that the modern day media regularly portray the impression that back then people tended to meekly tolerate their appalling quality of life with feeble resignation. Such misguided assumptions are rejected by anyone who actually lived through those times. There was constant pressure and numerous attempts to force politicians to address the problems by adopting radical policies; such pleas attracted little constructive response from those in power.

Other people point out that far from meekly accepting their circumstances it was the dreadful living conditions of that era that first inspired a determined grass-roots campaign to establish a comprehensive welfare state system so that future generations would never experience similar hardships.

Why a revolution was never contemplated in that era

Even in pre-war days, governments issued regular lists of statistics detailing certain trends in society – just as they do today. Predictably most people noted them with a great amount of scepticism because few believed the information even remotely reflected their own daily lives, merely serving as a convenient camouflage to conceal the truth.

They did sometimes provide useful details of certain aspects of people's lifestyles. For instance, the information that very few owned a car, only a tiny minority of homes had a telephone and the luxury of paid holidays was restricted to a very small section of the overall workforce.

Other statistics from that era reveal that the average weekly wage was £2 10*s*. A standard privately rented property cost around 4*s* 6*d*, while a new three-bedroom house could be purchased for something like £450 by offering a deposit of £40, and weekly repayments of 12*s* 6*d* over twenty-five years.

An interesting observation some people make about that period, is to pose the question: why no serious grass-roots revolution was ever contemplated during that era of widespread despair? One explanation offered is that for some reason people retained a stubborn, outmoded conviction that affairs of state were best left in the hands of the aristocracy and the establishment. This old-fashioned attitude partly explains why the only seriously organised challenge to existing authority, namely the 1926 General Strike, collapsed with nothing changed or gained.

In addition, there was the ever-present influence of disapproving religious leaders at a time when displays of public dissent against existing governments were considered to be 'not quite the English way of doing things'. Religion in general was a very powerful factor at the time to always discourage any such action.

CHAPTER FIVE

Social Reform and Working Lives

It would take over three more decades from the time of the Depression, before the scourges of widespread poverty and decay began to gradually subside. This improvement in the quality of people's lives was achieved by grass roots pressure and increased trade union activity – this resulted in a prolonged campaign to bring about wholesale social changes and reforms. One example was the struggle in the mid-1930s for a shorter working week under the slogan '8 hours work, 8 hours leisure and 8 hours sleep'.

The ultimate intention of this bloodless revolution was the establishment of an all-embracing welfare system for everyone. Throughout the Second World War, policies to establish better educational facilities to improve the daily diet for young and old, extend municipal health resources and the provision of free vitamins for children, helped the overall struggle to build a more just postwar society and bring about massive changes in old-fashioned social attitudes.

Before the outbreak of war, campaigners for social change had been rewarded with the passing of legislation in 1937 to provide secondary education for all, and also a further commitment was made to raise the school leaving age to fifteen. Unfortunately, the outbreak of hostilities meant that this additional proposal would be shelved until 1945.

The pressure to gain a fairer society continued unabated with men and women all over the Black Country attending meetings to lobby politicians to legislate for a better standard of life once the war ended.

Every member of the wartime coalition government became only too aware that when hostilities did end, people would never again accept thr conditions they had endured in the past. This message struck a chord with politicians of all three parties, resulting in the publication of the revolutionary Beverage Report in 1942.

Slater Street School, Darlaston, c. 1930.

Work and its once-dominant role in people's lives

To appreciate the harsh lifestyle of the early decades of the twentieth century, it is essential to try and evaluate all areas of society covering social attitudes, work, leisure and various beliefs. For thousands of ordinary working-class families, their lifestyle was a restricted repetitive daily routine devoted mainly to hard graft, with limited leisure opportunities, and very few luxuries of any description.

Finishing school on a Friday at the age of fourteen, a youngster was expected to start working for a living within a week. This inevitably involved a frenetic scramble to find immediate employment even if it meant taking a 'ten-a-penny' dead-end job to satisfy the standard Black Country philosophy, 'if yow dow work, yow dow ate', a sentiment everyone shared, and every school leaver was expected to follow.

With no welfare cover worth mentioning, work was all-important and any able-bodied person of working age who deliberately chose to remain unemployed would soon be labelled socially irresponsible by relatives, neighbours, and society as a whole. In keeping with this strict philosophy, late on a Sunday evening, all over the region, the entire local workforce would begin focussing on the coming working week. From Monday to Saturday lunchtime, the need to concentrate thoughts on earning a living would take over from all other considerations. Everyone just accepted the reality of facing another weekly round of low wages, long hours and unpleasant working conditions because it was the only way of paying the rent, buying food, purchasing essential clothes, and, with no free health service – settling doctor's bills.

The Monday morning struggle to prepare for work

Preparations for an early Monday morning departure to work would almost certainly have begun late on Sunday evening. Sandwiches would be made, overalls and other essential gear carefully laid out and shoes cleaned, all designed to ensure a quick getaway to the workplace on time. From first light there would be the noisy jostle to get dressed, shave, eat and make last-minute adjustments. For housewives, there would be the added stress of organising the Monday morning washday arrangements. The biggest priority for everyone was getting a fire going as quickly as possible because it was the only means of obtaining hot water for cooking, tea-making, shaving and washing. Such things as electric toasters, shavers or kettles were non-existent.

Whoever found themselves with the unpleasant chore of clearing out the previous night's ashes from the fireplace always needed to be careful during the process of removal not to spill any of the contents, otherwise the whole room would be filled with clouds of grey dust. All kinds of ingenious methods were used to light a fire in the shortest possible time. The most widely favoured was to place in the grate a number of small ready cut wooden sticks (kindling) extracted from a bundle brought from the local corner shop. On top of these would be added a few tiny balls of newspaper together with small pieces of coal. Finally, a match would be struck. In some households, old sheets of newspaper would be placed on to the front fire bars to try and create an upward draught and though effective, it was also a risky manoeuvre. Before long the newspaper would catch fire so the process needed to be closely monitored to prevent any fire falling on to the rug or carpet. An even more dangerous practice used to speed things up was to add a few drops of lamp oil. This lethal method worked, but there was always the possibility of a sudden blow-back of flames, and the prospect of someone standing nearby getting badly burnt.

For those living in any of the dilapidated Black Country slums there were even greater problems, particularly for large families arising from the additional stress of overcrowding, shared toilet facilities, outside water supplies, acute lack of space and, in the winter months, frequent overnight freezing. From the time a youngster left school and started to earn a living, this early-morning scramble became a priority of their everyday working life.

Stringent penalties imposed for bad time keeping

Once all the bedlam and bustle of trying to dress, wash, shave and starting the fire had ended, it was time to concentrate thoughts on the very important business of actually getting to the factory, office or shop. In this era of hardly any town-planning, many small industries happened to be situated close to residential areas, providing easy access to work for those living practically on the 'doorstep' of their work place. However, the vast majority of working people had to walk on average two miles a day to get to their factory or office – whatever the weather.

Hardly anyone owned a car and those who could afford the fare used the municipal bus service, which would be packed with workers from very early in the morning and in the evening taking people home.

Every local town possessed its own railway station and those who could afford to, would take advantage of the cheap rail fares, while others saved their hard-earned money to buy a bicycle. This form of transportation was popular throughout the region as the most convenient method of getting to work on time.

Good timekeeping was a matter of great importance because most employers carried out a vigorous policy of imposing financial penalties for 'clocking on' late. Some also imposed the severe rule of sending workers home for the day as punishment with the subsequent serious loss of a full day's pay. The impact of this could be witnessed in every Black Country town from Monday to Saturday, as the streets echoed to the sound of men and women, hurrying to work against a background of wailing works sirens. These would act as a reminder to workers of just how much time was left before they had to 'clock on' to avoid being penalised.

Lots of people, when reminiscing about their working lives, mention the important role of the factory siren and how it also became a vital timecheck for the whole family. As the monotonous tone reverberated over the rooftops, there would follow the daily spectacle of people running the final few yards to the factory gate because few could risk having their meagre wages reduced through bad timekeeping. This is perhaps the main reason why sirens were once such an integral part of the working week.

Harsh working conditions

Most firms expected its workforce to commence and finish their normal 5½-day working week at the precise time agreed when accepting the job. Casual conversation during working hours was totally discouraged and strict morning and afternoon tea breaks were enforced. It was not uncommon for workers to have to get permission from the foreman before going to the toilet. Colds, upset stomachs, bouts of migraine, or even a touch of influenza were all looked upon by management as being symptoms of a 'minor nature' – offering little excuse for absence.

Persistent absenteeism often resulted in dismissal with no system of appeal and with no union support – particularly in the thousands of small back-street factories. People simply endured the pains of these so-called minor ailments and reported for work rather than risk losing their job.

The foreman's word was law on the shop floor in enforcing all rules, regulations and discipline, so it was sensible and necessary to avoid offending them. Every employee was subject to the working practices of a firm without question if they wished to hold down a job. Even though the working environment was likely to be a mixture of dirt, grime, noise and polluted air, they were expected to endure the conditions without complaint.

Obviously circumstances were far better for those working for the large, world-renowned industries in the region. They provided protective clothing, works canteens, air conditioning, medical facilities, modern lighting and a whole range of health protection for their workforce.

Primitive working conditions were also applicable to women, especially those who worked on 'emery wheel' type machinery, which involved being persistently sprayed with nasty-smelling 'slurry oil' that not only soiled protective overalls, leaving a stain, but it also infiltrated exposed parts of the body, often causing complaints such as dermatitis. Many women emphasis that the unpleasant substance would leave a lingering aroma which necessitated a great deal of washing and scrubbing as soon as they got home, otherwise the smell would just persist. They would therefore wash their hair on a daily basis to prevent this happening.

There is little doubt that many of the awful working environments existing in Black Country factories and offices, up to the end of the 1950s, would have resulted in their automatic closure under modern day health and safety laws. Unfortunately, politicians displayed little concern or urgency to improve the situation during that period of time. This explains why thousands of men and women have suffered the trauma of various industrial diseases for many subsequent years of their lives.

CHAPTER SIX

Black Country Poverty and Sub-Standard Housing

In lots of households there would be the obligatory weekly jaunt to the local pawnshop to either redeem or pledge items of clothing or precious family possessions. During the Depression, it was a familiar sight to see moneylenders' premises, or pawnshops, flourishing on every street corner all over the Black Country. There are numerous accounts told of desperate housewives resorting to pledging their wedding rings, simply to ensure that there was at least one wholesome meal for her family in the middle of the week. This was especially so if she couldn't get anything more 'on tick' from the local corner shop because she was over her credit limit.

Pawnbroker, Five Ways, Stafford Road, Wolverhampton.

Housewives hated the humiliation of pawning clothes, shoes and any household ornament likely to attract a few shillings ticket value, but many had no alternative but to use this service. Women cringed at the mere thought of their neighbours witnessing these weekly trips to the pawnshop, even though the practice was widespread. Everyone was familiar with the well-known phrase of that era 'in on Monday, out on Friday', which meant that something such as the husband's only suit would be needed for the weekend to enable him to go out.

It was, however, a system that offered a temporary solution for thousands of poverty-stricken families during the long periods of mass unemployment and, at times, total despair.

The daily pressures of living in sub-standard housing

The wretched slum conditions endured by thousands of Black Country families throughout the early part of the twentieth century are now but a distant memory. It is nevertheless important that they are documented for posterity. Future generations need to know what it was like to exist in a household with limited space and the minimum of civilised amenities. Only those forced by financial circumstances to live in one of the numerous tiny sub-standard houses that scarred the local landscape, can accurately describe the impact such conditions had on people's lives.

The bulk of these 'jerry built' properties were constructed around 1868 in many instances, to accommodate the local workforce. Most small firms located in back-streets found a system of recruiting workers from the surrounding neighbourhood to be economically convenient. This policy also suited many local people because it avoided the cost and inconvenience of travelling to work, while also providing the opportunity of going home for lunch, an important factor at the time, when works canteens were few and far between.

Mostly this type of local low-cost accommodation was owned by what was known as 'absentee landlords' living well away from the area, and consequently with little interest in maintenance or general repairs. They were always content to place responsibility for weekly rent collection and repairs with local house agents who had little time for resolving tenants' complaints. Their priority was always the prompt collection of rent and, of course, their weekly collection commission.

Crooked Lane, off Stafford Street, Wolverhampton.

In every town, there were endless rows of neglected properties located alongside small factories that continually discharged poisonous pollution into the atmosphere, creating a dangerous and unhealthy environment. Those who grew up living in typical slum areas provide numerous accounts of leaking roofs, draughty windows with gaping holes, cracked walls, damp bedrooms, poor sanitation and for many the dreaded nightmare of being infested with cockroaches. In addition, there was the problem of sharing an outside toilet with

Edwards Road, off Dudley Road, Wolverhampton.

several other families and for those in a typical pre-war type courtyard, the added pressure of a shared 'brew house'. This meant taking turns on a rota system to use these primitive washhouse facilities to do the weekly wash.

Without doubt, the worst type of dwellings were the awful back-to-back properties, which had no internal water supply and frequently these cramped hovels housed two entirely separate families. One family would live in the front of the property and the other in the rear, with only a slim dividing wall between them. Even in that era of friendly neighbours there was always the problem of the slightest noise being clearly audible through the paper-thin wall. The absence of any type of privacy made it hard to avoid the occasional outbreak of friction.

During the bitter winter months, outside toilets and communal water taps would freeze up. Apart from the obvious difficulties these circumstances created it also meant there was no water for washing or making a drink. Some households attempted to anticipate any likelihood of frost by maintaining a low fire throughout the night. Before retiring to bed, salt would be sprinkled on the top of the coal fire, together with lots of slack and potato peelings to achieve a slow burn. Then a big kettle of water was filled and placed on the hob. This ensured a kettle full of hot water was available first thing in the morning.

Somehow, previous generations managed to overcome whatever daily domestic obstacles confronted them. It surely speaks volumes for their undoubted character and durability that they still retained a sense of humour. In spite of everything, most families kept in touch with each other after slum clearance, but greater efforts should have been made by those in authority to relocate families together, to ensure the continuation of their priceless neighbourhood spirit. Many older people regret this never happened and believe very strongly that during the immediate postwar years most Black Country councils adopted a typical bureaucratic approach when relocating families. By implementing a system of treating the problem as one of simply bricks and mortar, they ignored the inevitable social problems involved in moving people away from their local communities. This ensured the destruction of traditional neighbourhood loyalties.

As evidence of this, older residents recall that within weeks of being moved, people were so unhappy about being separated from their old familiar haunts and friends, they would go back visiting at every available opportunity. For some it was to attend their old place of worship, for others a favourite pub or club and a minority continued to go back to spend time with relatives or old neighbours who were still waiting their turn to be moved.

Consequently, those who saw for themselves what was happening to their communities in the 1950s are convinced that many of today's anti-social behaviour problems are partly the result of people no longer feeling that they are part of an identifiable close-knit neighbourhood.

CHAPTER SEVEN

Sights, Sounds and Images of the Black Country

From the beginning of the twentieth century, new industrial and commercial innovations began to change the character and environmental landscape of the Black Country forever. After the end of the First World War this process quickly accelerated with the spread of new manufacturing methods and new technical inventions, which changed many long-standing working practices and forms of transportation. This trend had an immediate impact on people's daily lives in all sorts of ways and the increasing use of mechanised vehicles being used to transport freight and goods soon began to threaten the region's long-established canal system.

Owing to the move away from using the canals, the area's waterways soon became commercially obsolete. Whole stretches became overgrown and choked with weeds and predictably ideal targets for dumping all kinds of rubbish even though the waterways had long been a vital part of the region's commercial lifeblood and a very important local social amenity.

The 1920s and '30s was an era when few working-class families could afford even a day at the seaside let alone a week's holiday. Consequently the nearest 'cut' provided a facility for people of all ages to utilise in their precious leisure hours. Every canal became an outlet for swimming, fishing, sailing model boats and on a Sunday, a noisy happy crowd would gather on individual bridges either engaging in one or other of those pursuits or simply watching the various activities while lapping up the sunshine. Most weekends whole families would occupy the grass verges near to the canal's edge to pitch a tent and have a picnic.

People who remember those scenes with great affection often refer to the problems of modern-day traffic gridlock and reflect on the fact that past

A typical boat family of the early twentieth century.

Victoria Basin, Broad Street, Wolverhampton. Canals were vital to Black Country trade and industry.

politicians and planners from that period displayed a total lack of foresight in allowing the region's canals to go into decline.

Thankfully, since the beginning of the 1970s, a belated but welcome attempt is being made to restore part of the waterways system to their former glory. It may well be that once again this cheap, pollution-free method of transportation will be utilised far more as an alternative means of commercial usage, and help to ease the ever-widening problem of daily road congestion.

Another early casualty of growing mechanised transportation occurred with the gradual disappearance of the much-loved horse and cart. They would meander daily down the back-streets making deliveries to shops and houses of all kinds of food, materials and goods. With its demise went the commonplace sight of children following horses and carts armed with a bucket and shovel to collect the manure left behind, which they would then sell to allotment-holders and neighbourhood gardeners for a few pennies.

The traditional Saturday morning sight of boys volunteering to assist the milkman, baker or greengrocer with his deliveries in return for a little extra pocket money and a chance to ride up front on the cart also vanished.

Another casualty was the colourful rag and bone man and his cart travelling up and down the side streets as he blew loudly on his horn, inviting youngsters to run home and bring back old clothing in exchange for a goldfish or balloon.

A further icon of the 1920s and '30s that fell prey to the relentless advance of modern transport was the majestic and powerful old-style steam roller. Just to witness those distinctive steam-powered giants of the road in action was a sight and sound never to be forgotten. Whenever one appeared in the neighbourhood

An early steam roller.

to repair a stretch of road, it would attract youngsters from far and wide simply to watch in awe, as they waited for the burning tar to be applied. Once the steaming hot tar had cooled down the children would move in to collect small pieces that had been left by the wayside when the steamroller moved on. These they would triumphantly gather up and take away to be slowly sucked at leisure like a lump of toffee. It was also considered to be a good method for cleaning the teeth. Just like the horse and cart, the unique sight and sound of those great breath-taking machines soon became rarer and rarer until by the late 1950s they were only to be found on fairgrounds providing power to drive various attractions.

Other major changes included in 1927, the first ever-public traffic lights appearing in Wolverhampton, followed by the publication of the Highway Code in 1931. During 1934, the standard driving test, which cost 7*s* 6*d*, became compulsory and a system of pedestrian crossings with the unique 'Belisha Beacon' (named after the Minister of Transport, Leslie Hore Belisha) became a familiar sight.

In that same year the number of vehicles on the roads topped the million and a quarter mark, and a 30mph speed limit was introduced for built-up areas. The motorcycle became popular, with a selection of models becoming available that ordinary families could afford. Among the most in demand was the Wolf 147cc, priced at around £18, together with the more expensive Sunbeam, which cost £46.

Owing to the increase in the volume of traffic, there were calls for great road safety legislation and so in 1935 the first 'cats' eyes' appeared on main roads in the Black Country. By then, twentieth-century technical and commercial progress had changed the old images, sounds and sights on roads and down back-streets in every local community.

Railway Casualties

At the start of the twentieth century, most Black Country towns prospered from having their own railway station, and many also operated an efficient goods and shunting depot. This facility was a boon to local manufacturing firms, mainly for the purpose of storing, receiving and transporting goods and materials on a daily basis.

Easy access to a passenger train made it possible for people to travel cheaply to destinations all over the country from their conveniently located town station and as a result, railway travel became very popular.

In addition people developed a strong fondness for the various companies that served the region; household names like GWR (Great Western Railway) or LMSR (London, Midland & Scottish Railways). The imposing sight and sound of those engines approaching a platform at a local station remains a life-long cherished memory for thousands who witnessed it. Families who lived close to a station with an adjacent busy goods yard – which would have operated flat out through the night – lived with the familiar clang and clatter of wagons being moved backwards and forwards. The noise of shunting must have made sleeping difficult for such families, but it truly was the golden age of steam.

The railway goods yard at Bilston Central.

The interconnecting railway network was always a great attraction. It was quite a common sight to see grown men standing on an overhead bridge gazing in awe as a magnificent express train thundered underneath, emitting clouds of thick smoke in its wake. A favourite hobby of youngsters was trainspotting, which involved the simple process of purchasing a platform ticket to sit for hours on a hard wooden bench collecting the individual numbers of trains as they entered and departed the platform. Enthusiasts would often stand on a railway embankment, usually with a supply of jam sandwiches and either a bottle of pop or cold tea, as they waited patiently for the opportunity to record each passing locomotive for inclusion in their prized album. It was a pastime that attracted a huge following, especially during the 1930s, creating a lucrative commercial market in magazines, books, catalogues, display cards and stickers – all devoted to the trainspotting craze.

Unfortunately in 1963 the whole network of stations and track became a target of the ill-conceived 'Beeching Plan' named after its author, Dr Richard Beeching. These proposals amounted to nothing more than a savage policy of dismantling mile after mile of track and the closure of numerous stations as part of a government cost-cutting exercise.

In spite of countless public protest meetings and petitions opposing the vicious cutbacks, the unpopular scheme was gradually implemented. As a direct result more and more freight was put on already inadequate roads and car traffic increased substantially, leading inevitably to the beginning of the appalling gridlock and road chaos of today.

One of the biggest ironies of that crazy policy is that planners and politicians have since spent millions of pounds of taxpayers money on schemes like the Midland Metro, built at a huge cost which ironically travels over almost the same route previously covered by the old Black Country railway system ruthlessly ripped up in the 1960s.

Black Country industry helps establish world land, sea and air records

In spite of the deep economic gloom of the Depression, in contrast it also proved to be a period of record-breaking in technical ingenuity, manufacturing and engineering that to a certain extent uplifted people's spirits. This was partly due to the fact that many of the land, rail, sea and air records achieved around that time were accomplished with the aid of the region's skilled workforce, confirming their wonderful reputation of producing whatever the business and commercial world required. It all helped to create a genuine feeling of pride among the working population.

Over a short period of time all types of world records were established and just as quickly surpassed at an astonishing pace beginning in 1930 with the unforgettable Amy Johnson's spectacular solo flight to Australia, quickly followed by her historic record-breaking dash to South Africa in 1932. These aviation exploits captured the public imagination and people clamoured to buy gramophone records, song sheets, miniature dolls, jigsaws and other types of souvenirs celebrating her achievements. It also created great public interest in all types of air travel and a much-needed upturn in the production of new fleets of passenger aircraft, from which many Black Country companies benefited enormously.

A similar trend was taking place on land with Malcolm Campbell in February 1931 shattering the existing speed record in his famous British built car Blue Bird. He reached an amazing speed of 245mph and went on to surpass that two years later, by clocking up 272mph. Finally on 3 September 1935, at Salt Lake Flats, Utah, he attained a breath taking speed of 304mph, breaking all existing speed barriers.

In addition, he broke the various water speed records with his powerful speedboat, Blue Bird K3. During that same era, the Singer Ten family car gained new speed records in 1931, but all of these milestones were overtaken by the performance of the awesome wonder car known as the Mobil Railton in 1938, driven by the legendary John Cobb attaining the then amazing speed of 350 mph. The special frame for the vehicle was made at John Thompson, Ettingshall, Bilston.

All through the 1930s, speed records continued to be surpassed both at sea and on the railways. Old people recall with pride the great ocean liners battling to smash the fastest Atlantic crossing time, achieved by the *Queen Mary*, an amazing ship that was launched in 1934. This performance was equalled by her sister ship, *Queen Elizabeth* in 1938. None of their commercial competitors could match either their speed or passenger luxury.

Because of the enormous interest generated by the battle to win the Blue Riband Atlantic crossing record, sea cruises became highly popular, with the average cost of a return trip to America being a mere £38. As this trend continued, there was an inevitable demand for more ships, increasing the need for specialised items manufactured in the Black Country.

Meanwhile, all sorts of advances were happening on the railways culminating in the 'Flying Scotsman' passenger train completing its daily London to Edinburgh run in a remarkable 7 hours 20 minutes.

Another area of manufacturing to profit from the continuing battle for extra speed and mobility, was that of motor cycle production, with local firms like Sunbeam and Triumph providing much-prized models for around £45. They became extremely popular with working-class families because it gave them access to the countryside and seaside at a reasonable cost. The clamour for new ships, cars, motor cycles, aeroplanes and trains, brought a greater economic prosperity for the region's skilled workforce.

From the comments of people who experienced the excitement of those unique record-breaking milestones, they felt proud to have made a contribution, however nominal, to the overall project.

Empire day parades

Memories still exist among elderly people of what they believed to be the sheer hypocrisy that once thrived in society, with particular reference to the traditional celebration of Empire Day on 24 May. For many it only revived memories of the numerous double standards associated with the pre-war era. They recall vividly all the humbug and public deception as they remember being marched around the school playground singing patriotic songs while waving Union Jacks in front of local dignitaries. Little consideration or thought would have been given to the fact that lots of children, particularly from the slum areas of the Black Country would have walked to their schools, having partaken of their meagre breakfast, usually consisting of a piece of bread with lard or butter.

Most would be wearing handed-down clothes. More than likely a fair proportion of boys would be dressed in trousers, which were little more than rags whereas others would have to go to school in shoes with pieces of cardboard to cover the holes in them for protection in bad weather. This state of affairs has been overlooked for decades, but serves as a graphic reminder of the low quality of life experienced by the poorer sections of society at the height of the Empire. This clearly demonstrates that ordinary people derived little benefit from the nation's extensive overseas possessions that formed the British Empire. Historians often disregard these facts when they debate the rights and wrongs of empire dominance. Without a doubt it brought many rewards for a privileged minority who would always have good reason for celebrating its existence and importance, but for the vast majority of working-class people, it did nothing to help alleviate their daily battle with poverty.

Street vendors

Before the spread of large supermarkets, housewives looked upon bartering with the various deliverymen and street vendors who traded their wares around every street, as just another part of running a home successfully. On top of the regular door-to-door service provided by the milkman, bread man, grocer, coal merchant and greengrocer, there were always the less-frequent visits by a salt seller, offering different sized blocks of salt for use as a preservative. On Fridays, it would be the

Chattin's horse-drawn delivery van outside the bakery in Bilston.

turn of the fresh fish man to make his appearance, offering a varied choice of fish from his wooden display boxes perched on his cart.

Then there was, of course, the knife-sharpener who moved from street to street pushing his specially adapted bicycle, fitted with a carborundum wheel, which was operated by foot pedal. He would happily sharpen any type of utensil for a small payment.

On winter Sundays, people would listen out for the welcoming shout of a bike-pushing vendor who had a large basket on the front covered in a spotless white cloth, hollering 'Get your lovely crumpets' – or pikelets as they were known locally. Then there was the fresh watercress seller who usually had a number of loyal housewives eager to make a purchase.

There was one tradesman more than any other who could guarantee a demand for his specialised services whenever he appeared in the area. This was the local chimney sweep. This demand would continue to flourish until the 1956 Clean Air Act, because up until then every Black Country dwelling relied on an open domestic fire requiring the chimney to be cleaned out on a regular basis for safety reasons.

Pritchard's milk delivery cart in Moxley.

The process of sweeping the chimneys would start with the placing of a large white sheet around the fireplace and hearth to minimise the possibilities of the room becoming covered with falling soot. Then a circular brush with a screw-fitting end would be attached to a number of extension rods by screwing them together one by one. This extended brush was gradually pushed up the chimney while being twisted from side to side until it finally poked through the top. After a thorough bout of brushing from side to side, it would then be carefully withdrawn by unscrewing each separate rod one at a time. This would cause great chunks of soot to come cascading down at regular intervals with the worried housewife anxiously looking on, hoping the bulk of it landed on the protective sheet.

Lots of people remember the messy and dangerous practice of 'firing' a domestic chimney, usually done to avoid the cost of employing a chimney sweep. Everyone was aware that it was actually against the law to attempt cleaning a domestic house chimney in this way. The process involved rolling pages of old newspapers into a number of small compact balls, which were then placed as far as possible up both sides of the chimney and set alight. Not surprisingly this created a fierce blaze inside the chimney, as it removed patches of firmly entrenched soot. Inevitably it also scattered dirt and dense smoke fumes from the chimney over the whole adjacent area, greatly annoying local neighbours.

CHAPTER EIGHT

Recession and Abdication

More and more signs started to appear within local communities indicating that the most severe economic and social impact of the 1930s depression were slowly receding. One obvious example of this welcoming trend could be ascertained from the increase in the number of Black Country households opting to have electricity installed. I well remember in 1936 my parents taking the decision to do so in our typical two-up two-down private rented property. In those days if a family made any sort of improvement to their house the tenant always paid with no contribution from their landlord. This possibly explains why we could only afford to install a supply of power to the two downstairs rooms and just the large bedroom, which meant continuing to use primitive candlelight in the remaining smaller bedroom on dark winter nights.

In Bissell Street, Bilston, where we lived, and in the surrounding neighbourhood area of Gozzard Street and Tame Street – which was a mixture of back-to-back and traditional slum properties – only a small minority opted to have electricity installed. It could only have been because of the lack of finance, considering the vast difference it made to living conditions. No more nasty-smelling lamp oil fumes or the constant need to change sitting positions to try to avoid the dark patches created by the old oil lamp suspended from the living room ceiling.

It also brought to an end the unpopular chore of traipsing along to the local lamp oil shop to purchase an essential weekly supply and, in the process, almost always managing to spill a certain amount of the smelly fuel on to parts of clothing.

The changing economic climate was also apparent from the marked increase in hire purchase business, which often caused friction in families, mainly because of a strong belief among some husbands that nothing should be purchased that could not be paid for from within the overall weekly income. One alternative method favoured by many housewives for solving the problem of providing for a special time of the year or a particular family event was to take advantage of the poplar 'credit cheque system' which thrived throughout the Black Country region between the 1930s and the 1950s.

Credit firms would provide regular cheques to the amount requested by a client, which could be exchanged at a number of nominated stores in return for chosen items. It was a system that gave families the opportunity of obtaining at short notice clothes, shoes and other necessities for occasions like weddings, funerals and inevitably Christmas, with all its added financial demands.

The specialist credit companies recovered their money through a fixed weekly instalment containing a small interest charge; this continued until the amount of the cheque had been recovered.

In certain homes, where the husband objected to any type of collection agent arriving at the door, it was quite common for a housewife to ask a sympathetic neighbour, who used the same collector, to also make her payment thus avoiding another possible domestic argument.

In 1935 Stanley Baldwin replaced the controversial Ramsay MacDonald as Prime Minister and it seemed that the most urgent problem on the horizon was the continuing expansion of German and Italian territorial demands. When Mussolini invaded Abyssinia the new Prime Minister responded by deciding to call an early election on the divided question of extended re-armament. This was held in November 1935 and his judgment was vindicated because his Conservative party obtained a comfortable majority of 246 over all others.

He immediately announced that it was his intention to present a full programme of rearmament to parliament early in the coming year. This proposed policy was dramatically overtaken by the sudden death of King George V in January 1936, an event that caused genuine grief throughout the Black Country region. Although it was known that he had been in poor health during the events held to celebrate his silver jubilee in May 1935, his death was still something of a shock to the nation.

Immediately Edward was elevated to succeed his father at the then age of forty-two. His youthful looks and apparent charm, attracted wide support and sympathy, which would however be very short. It appeared sources in the USA had been aware long before the British public of rumours about his association with a Mrs Wallis Simpson, a well-known American divorcee.

Apparently British newspaper proprietors had agreed to withhold any information on this sensitive issue, but the affair had become common knowledge amongst many of the nation's top establishment and when it emerged that Edward was determined to marry her, his position became more and more controversial and divisive making it no longer possible to keep it from the whole country.

A visit to stricken South Wales prompted Edward VIII to call for change.

In the event it turned out that many ordinary people openly supported his stance in spite of Prime Minister Baldwin proclaiming, 'the country will not stand for it'. A minority took the view that they should marry on the understanding that she would never be queen, others believed that politicians, and above all, entrenched religious leaders had combined to stop any proposed marriage.

One reason why Edward VIII attracted support revolved around an event that occurred during a two-day visit he made in November 1936 to Dowlais, a depressed town in the South Wales area. During the tour he was introduced to a group of miners and their families, all of them struggling to survive on a weekly pittance and living in appalling housing conditions. It appears the king was so moved by witnessing such poverty and squalor that he actually commented, 'Something must be done', four words captured by newspapers the following day.

Not surprisingly the whole incident increased his popularity and nowhere more so than in the Black Country, where so many experienced similar circumstances every day of their lives. Lots of people sent letters of support pleading for the Government to find an acceptable solution, but the Prime Minister finally informed Edward that marriage to Mrs Simpson would leave the king with no alternative other than abdication if lasting harm to the crown was to be avoided.

Farewell to Edward VIII and the new King is crowned

The final chapter of this controversial chain of events was played out on 11 December 1936, just 24 hours after the abdication of Edward VIII, when the outgoing monarch made his emotional farewell broadcast to the nation. Later that evening, he slipped quietly out of the country. In a clear effort to subdue any prolonged public anxiety, subsequent government announcements deliberately promoted the forthcoming coronation of his brother, George VI on 12 May 1937, emphasising how it provided a wonderful opportunity for stability and unity. In response, all kinds of manufacturers swiftly moved to produce their own type of souvenir which included chocolates, shaving mugs, boxes of biscuits, jigsaw puzzles, crockery, cigarette cards, ashtrays, tablets of soap, pencils and pens, books and magazines.

Local communities soon responded to this appeal for reconciliation with every town forming its own Coronation Celebration Committee to plan and organise a wide variety of public events and to encourage people to become involved. Looking back at a selection of those events, it's easy to see all the efforts made to make the occasion memorable for all age groups.

The programmes included parades, concerts, street parties, competitions, talent contests and all types of dancing. There were also firework displays and all manner of novelty shows. Enormous efforts were made to persuade and cajole shops, firms, public houses and every street to enter into the spirit of things by putting on colourful displays of flags and bunting and to hang eye-catching banners in support of the royal couple.

Almost inevitably, the weather was dull on the day, but by glancing back at proceedings in just three randomly selected towns, namely Wednesbury, Darlaston and Bilston, some idea of the excitement and enthusiasm of the occasion can be gleaned.

In Wednesbury the scheduled programme began with the distribution of a special Coronation payment to all the unemployed in the town that consisted of an extra 1*s* for single people and 2*s* to all unemployed married men. At 9.45 am, there was a procession through the town centre, comprised of local political dignitaries, members of the business community, religious representatives and groups from every voluntary organisation, plus the police, local magistrates and council officers. From the town centre they marched to Brunswick Park and assembled to hear a relayed wireless broadcast of the Coronation at Westminster Abbey at 11 am, and afterwards the mayor and others present planted a number of red and pink flowering commemorative trees, prior to the erection of an official plaque on the site.

From 2.30 pm in the afternoon in Wednesbury marketplace after another parade, mixed choirs and bands provided community singing and every pensioner living with in the borough boundaries was issued with a bonus gift voucher worth 1*s* 6*d* to mark the special occasion.

In Darlaston similar events and activities were held apart from minor differences; for instance all children up to the age of fourteen were given a coronation medal, and the local authority promoted a sustained campaign designed to persuade its residents to purchase patriotic red white and blue emblems made by local disabled ex-servicemen with the proceeds being donated to British Legion funds.

Throughout the day the parish church bells rang out in celebration, while at the town football ground a friendly challenge match between a team made up of local businessmen and one comprising well-known sportsmen and politicians was held which attracted a large attendance.

There was also continuous ballroom dance at various venues sufficient to satisfy every enthusiast, culminating in a spectacular floodlit municipal dance in the town's Victoria Park. Most streets put on family parties and huge crowds flocked to a variety of sports events and concerts, before finally congregating to watch an impressive fireworks display that was visible for miles around.

Meanwhile events in Bilston included a programme of processions, massed band rallies, a popular local talent contest, all types of sports games, ballroom

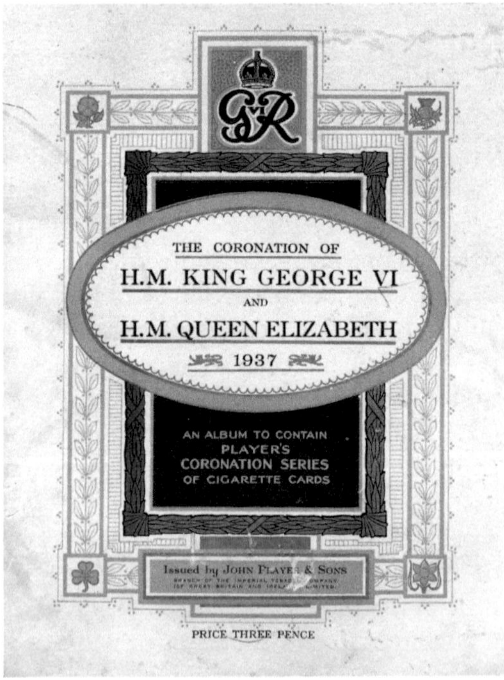

dancing and street parties. A novel variation involved a scheme to open an individual bank account for children born in the town during coronation week. To encourage parental participation in this novelty proposal £1 was donated from the mayor's charity fund and placed into an account with the Trustees Savings Bank on behalf of each newly born child.

Just a brief glance back at the announcement columns of the local newspapers of that month reveals that the choice of names for boys was George, and not surprisingly Elizabeth for girls; yet a further indication of the growing obsession for anything connected with that historic milestone in history.

Every pensioner in Bilston received a special one off payment of 2*s* 6*d*, while unemployed married men were given 3*s* and single unemployed 2*s* to mark the occasion. Each church and chapel organised their own form of entertainment, which included processions, concerts and fancy dress competitions. The whole town participated in a mass display of banners, flags and bunting and the day's festivities ended with a rousing firework display.

Most large stores in the Black Country contributed to the spirit of the occasion with special promotions offering free coronation gifts with each purchase. A famous furniture establishment in Dudley gave a specifically designed cutlery set to customers agreeing to furnish two bedrooms for a weekly payment of 5*s* on hire purchase

In Wolverhampton another large furniture outlet tempted people with a similar gift of a coronation linen basket if they purchased a three-piece bedroom suite using their hire purchase scheme of 2*s* weekly payments plus a complete dinning room set requiring weekly repayments of 2*s* 6*d*. Both of these examples are informative because they indicate the increasing attraction of buying on hire purchase.

Any lingering doubts about the rights and wrongs of the abdication began to gradually disappear locally amid all of the celebrations; but the former king and Mrs Simpson still appeared regularly on cinema newsreels, in magazines and newspapers.

On 27 May 1937, the Prime Minister Stanley Baldwin resigned and was succeeded by Neville Chamberlain, a development that shocked many people. Finally, the period of instability ended when Edward became the Duke of Windsor and then at last married Mrs Simpson on 3 June in France.

Increase in consumer spending and new industries come to the Black Country

The country over which the newly installed King George VI and Queen Elizabeth were to rule following the coronation, was in far better shape economically than had ever seemed likely at the beginning of the 1930s. Every sign indicated that in fact the king would inherit a nation undergoing a massive industrial transition, with large modern companies replacing old-style heavy industries. Nowhere was this dramatic changeover more evident than in the manufacturing heartland of the Black Country.

From the Depression, the entire economic and social framework of the region had slowly started to change. This involved new types of industries springing up all over the region producing plastic, chemical and electrical goods. The local workforce began to experience the benefits and this, in turn created a wider consumer demand which high street shops swiftly responded to by launching extensive advertising campaigns for clothing, furniture, household goods, wireless sets, portable gramophones and a whole range of new products.

It was a period when a pound in the pocket was considered a luxury, with inflation being practically non-existent between 1932 and 1938 and the price of food staying low, mainly because of cheap imports from Commonwealth countries during that period. Also a prolonged advertising campaign was started in newspapers, magazines and cinemas, with even large aeroplane banners used to persuade people to spend their increased incomes.

Another significant development was the introduction of cheap mass-produced clothes such as the popular 'made to measure' suits on offer at the local high street tailors for 50*s*. Many people recall the familiar 'off the peg' sports coats with matching trousers costing £1 10*s* and flannel trousers in a variety of colours, priced at the princely sum of 6*s*.

In the mid-1930s practically every town had a familiar Woolworth's store, trading under the well-known pledge 'nothing in this store over 6*d*' and providing a wide selection of goods to grateful housewives.

Over the years leading up to the Second World War, prices were also kept low because of keen-edged competition between traders, with emphasis being placed on courtesy, civility and a policy of the customer being right at all times.

CHAPTER NINE

Religion, Marriage and Death

Almost everyone in the early decades of the twentieth century followed a rigid code of Sunday observance with solemnity being of the utmost priority. This would be reflected in the closure of all high street shops, businesses and cafés. In addition, theatres, cinemas, dance halls and every other type of building offering public entertainment were also shut. Public houses only opened from 10 am to 2 pm and in the evening, from 7 pm until 10 pm. These rules were strongly enforced by local magistrates. In similar fashion, local corner shops were subject to limited trading hours prior to closing altogether at lunchtime.

There was a total ban on all forms of organised sport – be it racing, cricket, football or tennis – and youngsters playing any type of ball game were sternly discouraged by most parents. Indoors, all forms of card games for adults and even harmless knitting were frowned upon.

Many people when recalling those years refer to the sheer boredom of a typical Sunday and what they considered to be the repressive influence on society of the Lord's Day Observance Society – a very active minority pressure group. They were so committed that they actually launched a campaign against mixed bathing in the Black Country area (at the local swimming baths) and also in the late 1940s, during the battles to legally open cinemas on a Sunday, actually preached that visiting a place of entertainment on the Sabbath was in direct defiance of God.

From early morning, every Sunday there would begin the constant ringing of church bells summoning worshippers to all kinds of religious services. Few people who experienced those traditional Sundays are ever likely to forget them.

Sunday School Anniversary, Bilston Congregational Church, Oxford Street.

Another feature was the unusually quiet surroundings resulting from the total absence of weekday factory background noise, no rowdy voices of children playing boisterous street games and hardly any traffic – all of which meant a peaceful environment.

In every household, children would be dressed in their dreaded Sunday best, which further curtailed any serious leisure opportunities mainly because of the fear of soiling those special clothes with all the ensuing parental repercussions. Children from religious families would be expected to attend morning service and very often, Sunday school in the afternoon. It is interesting to note the findings of a survey undertaken in the region around this time, which disclosed that 83 per cent of the population regularly experienced this type of routine in their childhood.

It was undoubtedly an era when in every community the local church or chapel was the hub of people's daily lives in a way that would be unimaginable in modern-day society.

This was particularly the case for Catholics who were subject to strict religious rules and regulations such as having to seek the permission of the local parish

Wesley Chapel. Spring Head, Wednesbury. (Reproduced by permission of Sandwell Community History and Archive Service)

priest before attending any non-Catholic service of any description. It applied to weddings, funerals and christenings and for service men and women the state allowed special dispensation for members of that faith to fall out of parades during the period of non-Catholic prayers, and then fall back in after they had concluded. Similarly, at all civilian functions, a practising Catholic would drop out of the proceedings that included any form of non-Catholic worship and rejoin the parade or celebrations afterwards.

Any form of mixed marriage required the non-Catholic partner to attend a course of religious instruction once a week for a period of three months and also instructions on how to bring up children in the faith. There are still many recollections retained by men and women who experienced these required undertakings first-hand and the often-inevitable resentment and misunderstanding they created. Thankfully such hard and fast rules have all but disappeared, and nowadays the various religions partake in each other's varied services in a way previous generations would never have believed possible.

A vivid indication of the impact of religion on communities was that of thriving Sunday schools with over 55 per cent of Black Country children attending this type of afternoon worship on a regular basis. They also taught reading and writing, organised day trips, seasonal parties and above all, the obligatory annual Sunday school celebrations and street parade. Accompanied by parents, each Sunday school would walk in procession around neighbourhood streets led by a Boys' Brigade or Scout band. Such parades would be quite large and always created a lot of excitement as the numerous banners and flags were carried past with great pride, backed up by adults rattling collection boxes, the spectators lining the streets cheerfully contributing their coins.

The children walked behind the band with girls wearing white dresses and the boys in smart white shirts. For this special occasion, mothers went to great lengths to ensure they also had a display of bows and ribbons for added decoration.

Each Sunday school operated a weekly attendance card system by awarding a star, and every child attaining a full set would receive a book prize as a reward at the end of the year. Another feature of the strong religious influence in the Black Country area was the importance attached to having a newborn baby christened within a specified period of days. Most adults, be they regular churchgoers or not, observed a strict Sabbath code of practice that barred any recreational activity and all forms of physical work of any description inside the household.

On the following Monday morning many church schools would actually question pupils about any absence from Sunday service and a weekly visit by clergy to ask questions about religious doctrine was a normal practice in those days.

Funerals

Throughout the early part of the twentieth century, a seemingly fixed ritual was followed whenever a death occurred. This revolved around the traditional etiquette of black armbands being worn by every close member of a family up until the day of funeral; curtains would be drawn, often mirrors were draped with strips of black ribbon, and the corpse was washed, dressed, and laid out in an open coffin. Afterwards it would be placed in the back room, providing the opportunity for friends and neighbours to call and pay their final respects.

As a child of thirteen, I experienced this macabre routine first-hand after losing my mother suddenly in the early 1940s. For some considerable time, people arrived from all over the neighbourhood to file past the coffin, which was in the front room surrounded by lighted candles, because that was the accepted way of doing things in those days.

Most people were buried in the local cemetery up until the end of the First World War, when as a result of the enormous amount of carnage and wholesale loss of life, overall attitudes changed and there was a definite increase in cremation; apart that is from the Catholic Church, which continued to retain strong objections to cremation.

B. Crowther, undertaker. (Reproduced by permission of Sandwell Community History and Archive Service)

All funeral services were extremely sombre with only limited references to the achievements, character and past life of the departed. A local senior citizen, reflecting on the occasion in the late 1940s when she attended the funeral of her grandmother, provides a clear example of the standard formula.

She especially remembers how the immediate family and close associates were expected to dress in the appropriate manner, and being from a fairly poor household, had no alternative but to ask around other relatives and neighbours to borrow the clothes and shoes necessary for the occasion.

This was a commonplace situation for most poor families whenever an unexpected bereavement occurred because of the financial problems created by having to purchase acceptable attire for the funeral. Many households tried to anticipate this scenario by taking out a small insurance cover known as a 'Death and Dividend' policy for a few pennies a week on various members of the immediate family – solely to avoid such an embarrassing situation occurring.

All along the route to church or chapel and cemetery, men would stop and raise their hats and women would pause in respect as the hearse passed by. After any interment it was customary to invite people back to the house for light refreshments, tea or a beer, but throughout the process the general environment would be restrained and mournful. Mourners would arrive back home to rooms with drawn curtains, and an overall atmosphere of restrained conversation, during which it seemed an act of virtual sacrilege to even smile. Nowadays the way funerals are conducted throughout the region has totally changed. People no longer feel obliged to attend wearing black and all kinds of popular music seem to be appropriate to mix with traditional hymns.

Everyone involved with the service of whatever faith now includes a tribute to the life of the deceased and gives a detailed portrait to the congregation. Even the odd joke emerges, and relatives and friends frequently read out poems. In addition, the Catholic Church have long ceased their opposition to cremation for the obvious reasons of lack of burial space, and it has become more and more popular for non-religious people to opt for a plain ceremony without religious content. This consists of a mixture of readings, poems, and personal tributes from friends, colleagues and relatives. This fresh approach to death in whatever form, is vastly different to what previous generations of Black Country men and women thought to be the right and proper way of saying goodbye to loved ones.

Such a liberal, open attitude would have been unthinkable to our grandparents and parents but thankfully they are now the accepted format.

CHAPTER TEN

Daily Life and Hardships

Everyday problems created by persistent industrial pollution.

Before the passing of the Clean Air Act in 1956, Black Country housewives had to cope daily with the problems caused by both persistent industrial pollution and domestic fires which regularly contaminated curtains and windows, and covered freshly washed clothes and sheets hung out to dry with grime and soot.

Such frustrating circumstances became even more acute during the long summer months with the necessity to maintain a fire for essential cooking and heating water. On really hot days the combination of a muggy polluted atmosphere plus a fire resulted in a stifling living room environment that at times would become almost unbearable. The only remedy was to throw open the living room window but this inevitably let in added dust and grime and the usual cluster of flies and other insects.

For anyone employed in a factory or foundry that had no air conditioning to speak of and a working area of unrelenting heat with precious little fresh air,

The Patent Shaft Works, Wednesbury, in the days when air pollution went unchecked.

found working conditions became unbearable. This typical sweatshop environment ensured they went home feeling totally drained and worn out. Not surprisingly, upon returning home covered in sweat they would immediately go outside to the brewhouse for a cool, refreshing wash down and afterwards look forward to a traditional Black Country meal.

In those days, for anyone working in heavy industry, such things as a cold salad or something similar would be looked upon as being totally unsuitable following a long day of hard toil. This meant housewives had no alternative but to cook something hot however unsuitable the weather may have been. It was a time when everyone believed it was essential for working men in particular, to have a least one such meal a day containing the right amount of fats and proteins to maintain their strength.

One of the most graphic and darkest images of the region was undoubtedly the daily railway journey from Wolverhampton to Snow Hill, Birmingham. The local trains would progress through Priestfield, Bilston, Wednesbury, West Bromwich, Handsworth and Soho, then in to Snow Hill. The sight that would greet passengers was a truly depressing one, typical of the old Black Country. Vast areas of the embankments would be strewn with industrial rubbish, old tyres and scrap vehicles, together with great stretches of stagnant canals – the whole environment shrouded in smoke, dirt and grime. This was a lasting impression visitors to the region took away with them. Few could understand why anyone could be so proud of their region and live in such an unpleasant environment.

Traditional corner shops and their role within the community

Those with memories of yesterday's Black Country will readily testify to the fact that even with their unhygienic health standards, the old-fashioned back street corner shops were the central linchpins of every community. Apart from trading in just about every known commodity imaginable, they also functioned as an early type of citizens' advice bureau and social services establishment. They provided locals with all forms of information and up-to-date news on forthcoming marriages, births, deaths, current domestic scandals, engagements, all types of petty crime and above all a searching appraisal of any newcomers moving into the surrounding neighbourhood.

Usually open all hours, they were a vital facility, and conveniently located, which was an additional bonus because for various reasons, housewives had no option but to shop every day. At that time when running a home was a full-time occupation, daily shopping expeditions gave them a brief respite in which to exchange gossip, views and information, while making their purchases.

Mostly these shops were nothing more than crudely converted standard two-up, two-down houses, with the front room containing the counter and lots of stacked shelves. Most pre-war back streets would have two or often three, all competing for the same local custom.

The majority operated a system of allowing weekly 'strap' and during the Depression this provided an indispensable service to thousands of desperate housewives, especially in the middle of the week when they would often run out of ready cash.

It was a system used extensively during the period of the notorious 'means test' and was a vital lifeline not available in the larger high street shops. Every local shopkeeper knew all of their customers and allowed food to be purchased 'on tick' with a clear understanding that all outstanding debts would be cleared come Friday pay night.

Low standards of hygiene in back street shops

Primitive hygiene standards were always the norm in most corner shops, and this fact seems to confirm the widely held view that older generations developed some form of inbuilt immunity against many known diseases, caused by eating contaminated food. With a complete absence of refrigeration or adequate food storage facilities, food contamination was a real threat to public health.

In addition, hardly any corner shop possessed running water and a sink for regular washing of hands. Normally the only water supply would be situated in the outside brew-house. As a consequence, numerous accounts of poor hygienic conditions exist from those years.

People recollect incidents of shopkeepers handling perishable food, while balancing a cigarette on the end of their lip which inevitably meant that a certain amount of ash dropped directly on to the serving area. This is a far cry from modern day no smoking regulations. Many also remember the scores of flies during the hot summer months, buzzing to and fro around the shop, posing a constant threat to any exposed food.

Without refrigeration, the only remedy was to hang strips of dark brown flypaper in prominent positions. The paper was coated with a solution of arsenic, sufficient to stun an insect immediately it got caught on the sticky surface before eventually dying. The problem increased with the daily delivery of fresh cream cakes, which would always be placed on prominent display to attract quick sales, which only made things worse. Sometimes the frustrated shopkeeper would respond by waving around a fly swatter in a vain attempt to deter them. In addition, lengths of muslin fabric would be used to cover the more perishable foods, but it was always a losing battle.

Often situated at the end of the serving counter was an area containing a marble slab for cutting meat, cheese, butter and other such products. The most

A typical Black Country butcher's shop.

popular size was 2oz portions, but in some cases the housewife would just ask for a single slice of meat for 'the old man's tea'.

Most shopkeepers wasted nothing; they would even scrape off the green mouldy part of the cheese and sell the remaining portion to some unsuspecting customer. It was also common practice to serve dirt-covered vegetables or even lamp oil within the same area and then just wipe their hands on a well-used teacloth before serving another customer with meat, butter or cheese. This only added to the risk of contamination.

Amazingly, the potential health hazards appeared to have little impact on the majority of people, endorsing the theory that people developed an immunity to most mild bacteria-related illnesses.

In addition, whenever the weekly budget allowed, housewives would purchase what they considered to be essential, wholesome food, but in reality it contained all types of fatty substances that nowadays would be classed as unhealthy by modern medical opinion. Such claims are often dismissed as rubbish by senior citizens of today who emphasise that every supermarket sells its share of trashy, tasteless junk food that amounts to a far greater health risk.

They also point out that continuous warnings by so called health gurus about eating the wrong type of food only encourages people to develop hang-ups about what they should or shouldn't eat for their own good.

Food contamination

It was not only shopkeepers but also every household that had to cope with the daily difficulties of food hygiene. For those living in cramped back-street slums, it was an even greater headache, especially for large families, because of acute overcrowding which created added difficulties of food preservation. Without the luxury of refrigeration in most homes, the problem would be partly solved by placing things like milk in a bucket of cold water, and in lots of small properties there was usually a cellar with a handy opening in the wall, which could be used to store certain types of food that would otherwise perish if left in a hot kitchen. This would be mainly butter, cheese and fruit; while in most households, meat would be placed in what was known as a 'meat safe' specifically designed for protecting it from going off.

One of the great drawbacks with using a cellar for this purpose was the fact that often it would be the only space for storing the coal, which invariably meant that when the weekly supply was off-loaded, the entire area would be covered in flying clouds of dust. Another factor was the necessity of maintaining an open fire in the living room for cooking and heating water; this increased the oppressive heat, to the extent that it could become almost stifling.

The only option was to open the door or windows encouraging flies into the room, which for some unknown reason seemed to be far more numerous than they are today. People relied heavily on the traditional deterrent of sticky flypaper. Before long, these strips of paper would be saturated with a mass of black flies. Some would be dead; others would be only half-dead and quite often a trapped victim managed to wriggle free of the gluey substance and fall directly on top of the exposed food on the table below. It was a period when few families could afford to throw away precious food, so when this happened the insect would be immediately dispatched by a parent with a dismissive sweep of the hand and the usual comment to 'Just ignore the pests and carry on eating.' Little sympathy would be shown to anyone displaying a reluctance to do so.

There would occur numerous incidences that people recall of flies detaching themselves from the overhanging flypaper, dropping straight into a cup of tea. The problem would swiftly be resolved by removing it, with the nearest spoon with the remark, 'It's still perfectly drinkable. A small fly can't do you any harm.'

Today's younger generation must find such incidents from the past difficult to comprehend. The idea of not throwing away food that had obviously been contaminated must seem unbelievable. In modern society the standard response would be to deposit the item swiftly into the waste bin. That was never an option in the majority of working-class homes. People accepted circumstances such as a fly landing on food and treated it as nothing more than an inconvenience, not worth making a fuss about.

In very poor working-class households, children refusing to eat anything put before them meant that they would go hungry until the next mealtime, because nothing else would be available in its place.

Public health in 1920s–40s

A major factor relating to the pattern of daily life from the start of the twentieth century was undoubtedly the extremely poor quality of most public health facilities. What medical care did exist was usually sketchy, and because it came with an appropriate charge, it was always a financial problem for those families already living from hand to mouth. It became the custom for many to depend solely on the good nature, charity or social conscience of their local 'panel doctor' when members of the family became ill. In many circumstances, the doctor was well aware that the particular family couldn't pay the full cost of the treatment and he would most likely accept a token payment or simply overlook it altogether. Doctors also accepted payment in kind, for instance, home-grown vegetables.

This type of caring attitude also extended to the district nurses, who worked tirelessly within their respective communities. This concern for the more unfortunate in society was also a feature of the hospitals that served the Black Country. These public institutions existed on shoestring incomes, made up mainly of voluntary donations throughout the year. These consisted of regular hospital flag days, which directly appealed to the generosity of ordinary people. Enthusiastic volunteers undertook essential fund-raising activities.

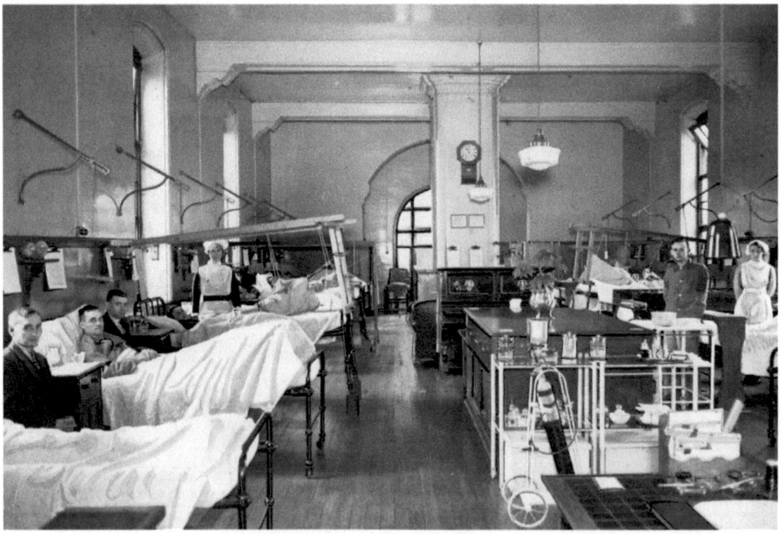

The Royal Hospital, Wolverhampton.

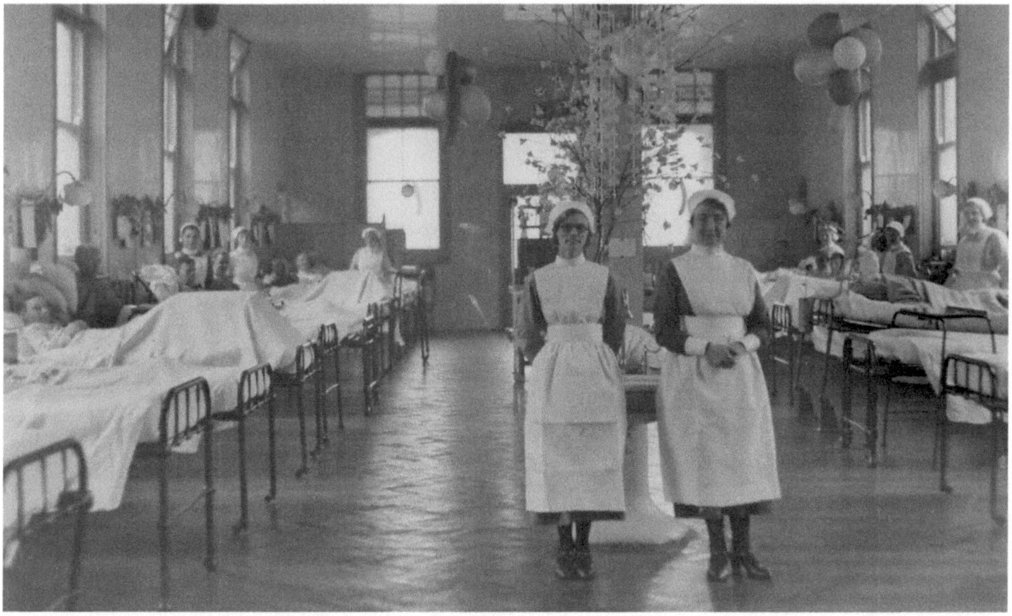

Nurse Manford (left), at New Cross Hospital, Wolverhampton, Christmas 1935.

Local communities fostered a great amount of pride and admiration for their particular hospital, and recognised the efforts and dedication provided by the staff working in the unique voluntary system of that period.

Home remedies

Prior to the emergence of a whole variety of new drugs in the second part of the twentieth century to counteract the threat from tuberculosis, pneumonia and other life-threatening sicknesses of those years, some of the more popular remedies were very primitive. Many people still retain vivid memories of one such crude form of treatment, dating back to the mid-1930s, for pneumonia, which often began as mild bronchitis before developing into this dangerous illness.

The standard treatment was the traditional remedy of applying what was known as a hot kaolin poultice. This was a strip of flexible brownish material containing kaolin (china clay), which had tiny holes in it. It was carefully placed on the chest and back of the patient with the aid of a paste type mixture (mustard plaster). It was customary to leave it on for a certain number of days to ensure the patient retained a constant temperature.

When the time came to remove the poultice, it was a very tricky and smelly procedure. There was always an over-powering odour in the room from the poultice and it caused agonising pain when it was removed with parts of the flesh coming away as the plaster was peeled off. Thankfully such remedies were later replaced rendered obsolete by the discovery of modern drugs.

An interesting factor relating to standards of health before 1939 disclosed that despite the appalling living and working conditions, cancer and heart disease were far less evident than they are today.

Every Black Country town suffered from lethal industrial pollution, which was a mixture of smoke, fumes, dust, grime, dirt and soot. In the wintertime, when this combined with the smoke emitted from thousands of open domestic fires, it became a dangerous health problem. On days of thick fog, everyone, especially the elderly or infirm who suffered from any type of bronchial complaint, would be extremely vulnerable outdoors. The polluted atmosphere created what was known as winter smog, which everyone dreaded.

People were always fearful of being absent from work owing to illness and many became fanatical about the general health of the family and went to great lengths to avoid any type of sickness. All types of old-fashioned remedies were used including a rigorous routine of cleansing the system to avoid constipation,

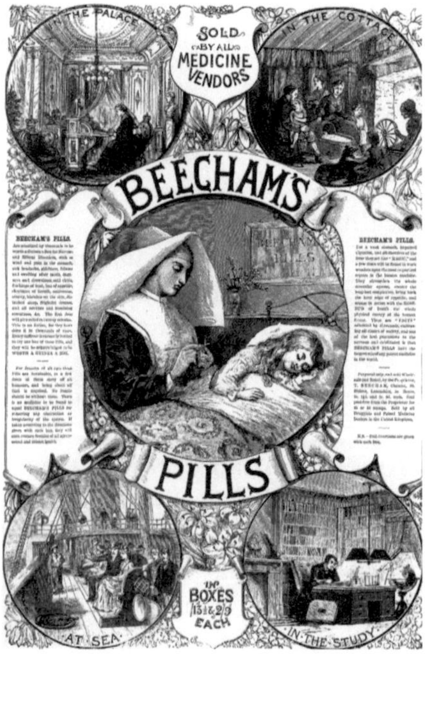

Cures for any ailment were readily available.

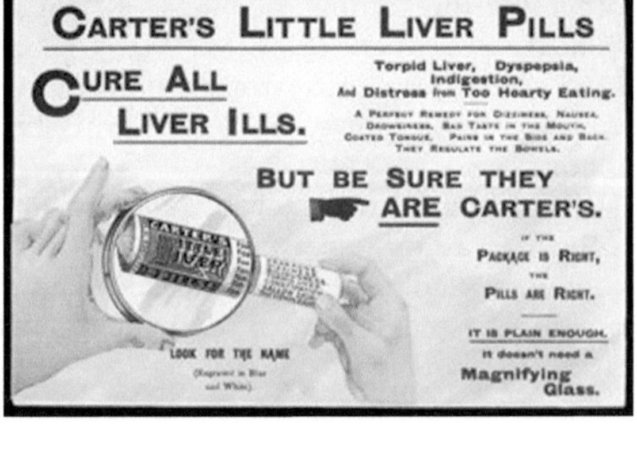

stomach complaints or other minor ailments. The need to 'always keep the bowels free' as the quaint local expression described it, became something of a fixation in many households.

This health mania was greatly encouraged by commercial firms flooding the high street shops with all types of pills, powders, tablets and salts that claimed to offer a whole panacea of cures for every type of illness.

They funded massive advertising campaigns using cinemas, newspapers, magazines and every available high street hoarding. People remember how they almost always featured the obligatory happy smiling housewife proclaiming how her family's overall health had improved from using a particular well-known product.

Because of the poor diet of that period, many people, especially women, experienced ulcerated legs and cellulites. A popular remedy was a very smelly mixture of glycerine and icthymol, which would be mixed together to form a paste, and then it would be spread on a clean piece of cloth and put on the open wound.

During the war there were regular five-minute broadcasts made by the Radio Doctor (Dr Charles Hill), that always included helpful tips and advice. These popular programme slots attracted a huge following throughout the Black Country area and they always concluded with a reminder to everyone to ensure their bowels were operating as they should. Older residents can recall being asked by a fussy parent before leaving for school on a morning if they had their bowels open beforehand.

Certain sections of the medical profession in the 1920s and '30s attributed many instances of constipation, stomach pains and bouts of severe headaches to the fact that the majority of working class households consumed far too much starchy, fattening food, which was very damaging to a person's overall health.

Others pointed out that it was not simply the diet of families, but also the primitive standards of hygiene, poor housing and limited public health resources that contributed to the problem.

Such conditions would be unthinkable in modern-day society, which leaves unanswered the intriguing question as to why with all the improvements in living and working conditions there appears to be no significant decrease in the number of cases of heart disease, cancer or other lung complaints such as asthma? With reduced industrial pollution, draconian food hygiene regulations, smokeless zones and a ban on smoking in public places, it seems logical to expect to see a major improvement, but this has simply not happened.

There are many who believe that the reason why people could consume food that had possibly been exposed to all types of germs and contained large amounts of starch and fat was because over the years they had evolved some form of immunity against food poisoning and other health hazards. Considering today's incessant warnings about the dangers of certain foods, this theory seems very plausible.

Food for working men

Previous generations were convinced that certain types of food were a necessary part of a healthy constitution, required by anyone working in the harsh conditions always present in local foundries and other types of heavy industry. Most working environments were a mixture of unhealthy pollution, dirt and noise and often primitive ventilation, usually limited to someone opening a window or door now and then. The workforce would be required to tolerate these dreadful conditions for the then average 49½-hour working week.

These long hours in such conditions would continue into the late 1940s before a significant reduction in hours was achieved with a gradual move towards a shortened 44-hour week. This concession would take some time before it became the accepted norm for all of the working population.

The importance of meals containing substantial strength-building ingredients was a conviction shared by most of the manual workforce who firmly believed they should include every type of food that is now widely condemned by modern-day food experts and dieticians.

Pigs' feet: a popular local delicacy.

This would include large quantities of things like fatty bacon, meat, lard, butter, potatoes, eggs, black pudding, faggots, rabbit, pigs' feet, bread pudding, spotted dick, jam roll, the ever-favourite 'chitlins' (cows' or pigs' intestines cleaned and cooked by the butcher), and just about every type of pastry-based concoction imaginable.

Bearing in mind the wide popularity for this type of food in the majority of households, a surprisingly strongly-worded report in 1930, published by the Midlands Sanitary Inspectors' Association directly criticised the eating habits of the region causing widespread controversy.

This official publication concluded that a large proportion of Black Country inhabitants were being 'slowly poisoned by the type of food they regularly consumed,' which was 'diluted with drugs in the guise of preservatives, causing a type of dope reaction among certain age groups depending on the amount eaten.'

These comments and observations were strongly endorsed by the Dudley Medical Officer of Health, who further remarked that it had become 'a common practice in the region to hoodwink consumers into buying doctored food,' and that 'it was not in the least surprising that frequent epidemics of mild illnesses occurred.'

Such a contentious statement made by someone so closely involved in overseeing the health of local communities seems all the more remarkable considering the appalling levels of hygiene flourishing in back street corner shops which was quietly ignored by those in authority.

The husband as the bread-winner

Only a very small minority of married women went out to work in the pre-war era. Those who did would generally do a few hours' office cleaning or helping out in a local shop, while others would take in other people's washing for a tiny remuneration. This was mainly to supplement the frugal family budget and was always kept to a minimum of hours simply because of the strongly held views of most men of that period who believed in the traditional philosophy that a wife's place was in the home, cooking, cleaning, shopping and looking after the children.

Most husbands contended that if his wife was forced to also go to work it was a direct reflection on his ability to uphold his family responsibilities and this masculine attitude meant most women were completely dependant on their husband's weekly wage. It also ensured that a housewife had precious little personal independence and constantly struggled on a financial knife-edge week after week making sure every precious penny was spent wisely.

If the husband and sole provider was taken ill, the whole household would be in a financial crisis before very long, because help from the state was very limited.

Fortunately this type of outmoded thinking regarding working married women was destined to change forever during the Second World War when a conscripted female workforce became an essential part of the battle for victory, ensuring that the old-fashioned notion of a husband being the sole provider became part of the area's history.

Typical weekly domestic chores

Housewives throughout the 1920s, '30s, '40s and most of the 1950s experienced a humdrum weekly routine of domestic chores, which included cleaning, cooking, sewing and essential daily shopping.

With none of the helpful labour-saving devices that are readily available in modern-day society, the routine involved a heavy schedule of very physically

Sweeping the yard: one of the many weekly chores. Alice Hasketh (née Fisher), Walker Road, Blakenhall, Walsall.

tiring tasks – none more so than the Monday washday. Memories abound of that testing chore which would normally commence around 6 a.m. in a typical outside brewhouse which was a small, roughly constructed building usually containing no door, numerous holes in the roof, with practically every window missing and in the corner, a traditional brick boiler.

Monday was washday. Pictured here is Lawyers Field, off Stafford Street, Wolverhampton.

For those who had a communal courtyard that only possessed one shared wash area (serving three or more families), there was always the extra problem of keeping to a strict allocated time schedule every week.

During bad weather, the exposed entrance of most of these brewhouses meant the floor would be swiftly saturated with rain or snow. To combat this annoying problem, many women resorted to wearing strong rubber wellies to keep their feet dry. The first task on any washday was to light a fire under the boiler, using small pieces of chopped wood and then adding tiny chunks of coal before applying a lighted strip of newspaper. No sooner was the fire lit, the surrounding area would rapidly be filled with smoke fumes, creating a quite unpleasant atmosphere for a time.

After filling the boiler with water, all items to be washed would be placed into a dolly tub, which was a large rounded wooden container into which the boiling water would be transferred. A sprinkling of soda would be added and then the hard work would begin to get the clothes clean. They would then have to be pounded repeatedly with a large wooden instrument known as a dolly.

Without fail, a proportion of the popular Reckitt's Blue was used to obtain a brighter wash. After washing, the clothes would be dipped in a mixture of Robin's Starch and water to stiffen shirts, collars, tablecloths and pillowcases.

The clothes were then put through an iron-framed contraption called a mangle. This had two large wooden rollers that squeezed out excess water from the washed item by slowly turning a very heavy iron wheel. After that they were rinsed in clean water and then mangled again. It was a strenuous back-breaking job for a woman.

If it wasn't raining, the completed wash would be placed in a basket and taken out into the yard and hung on a clothes line, using wooden pegs and finally a wooden prop would be placed under the line to stop the clothes from dragging on the ground.

On any washday the circumstances guaranteed to cause a housewife the greatest frustration would be inclement weather, resulting in the massive problem of where to hang all the wet clothes in the limited space available of a tiny two-up, two-down house of that era. Every corner of the small living room would have been utilised and apart from the unpleasant smell of slowly drying clothes drifting around the room, there was also the additional problem of how a housewife would get access to the fire in order to cook family meals.

The situation was not helped by the fact that every home needed to have a large wooden table for eating purposes. This further restricted the amount of room for manoeuvre, so it was little wonder that the prospect of rain on a Monday was something housewives dreaded.

The final job was to clean out the boiler and get rid of the ashes before scrubbing the brewhouse floor using a hard brush and soapy water and then using the remaining soapy water to wash down the outside yard. Although the old-fashioned method of washing was always very exhausting, women nevertheless took great pride in making sure every item sparkled with cleanliness, be it family clothes, bed linen, table clothes or merely handkerchiefs.

In most households, Tuesday would be set aside for ironing. This was a chore which was also physically demanding on housewives because it meant having to use two old-style heavy flat irons that were made of cast iron. Both would be placed on a metal support fixed to the bars of the domestic fire, known as iron strides. When it was judged to be the right moment, one would be removed after carefully wrapping an old piece of cloth round the handle to protect the hand from a possible burn. Then, before ironing commenced, the housewife would spit on the bottom to make a distinct sizzling noise. This was done to confirm the right heat had been reached. When completely satisfied she would begin the laborious process of ironing – no easy task, especially for anyone frail.

There was also the tiring necessity to regularly interchange each iron as it cooled and replace it with the one left on the strides to heat up. When every item

A group of 1930s Black Country housewives enjoying a brief break from the chores. (Reproduced by permission of Sandwell Community History and Archive Service)

had been ironed they would be put in a large basket before being stacked in a cupboard ready for use.

For many families, Wednesdays would be set aside for the thorough cleaning out of bedrooms. With no vacuum cleaners available, there was no alternative but to get out the dustpan and brush and apply a lot of hard graft. Also every household had to cope with the problem of emptying full chamber pots and then cleaning them with an application of soda water or some other type of cleansing substance.

All carpets had to be hauled outside and strung over the washing line and then given a brisk beating to remove any dirt before being taken back into the house. Floors and the front door step would be vigorously scrubbed with a hard brush and soapy water. The large living room table also received a weekly scrub down and the collection of brass ornaments that decorated every home were polished to perfection.

Most housewives liked to set aside Thursdays for doing extra cooking. Many favoured lots of wholesome home baking, such as making apple pies, bread pudding, rhubarb pies, seed cake, jam sponge and various other popular concoctions of home cuisine.

In most homes, Friday was the preferred day of the week for doing the unpleasant, dirty and tiring job of black-leading the fireplace, regarded by many women as the most important domestic job of the week after washday. Even on cold winter mornings, no warming fire could be started until the whole process of black-leading had been completed. The polish was purchased in a round tin and required mixing with water to form a kind of paste. A liberal amount would be applied to the whole fireplace using a special brush, which had a wooden handle for gripping tightly. There was vigorous brushing into every corner and crevice. Finally a rag would be used for intensive polishing until it shone to a satisfactory level.

The majority of women believed this weekly ritual should be carried out thoroughly because the fireplace was regarded as the focal point of any home; making it very important that it caught the eye of any visitor immediately they entered the living room area. This preoccupation to ensure it always shone was important to housewives right up until the demise of the domestic fire in the mid-1950s when gradually they would be replaced by modern gas or electric appliances.

Usually Friday was also designated as bath night especially for thousands living in properties with no bathroom. Throughout the acute postwar housing shortage, most people regarded the facility of a private bathroom as a far-off dream. This was particularly so for newly married couples anchored at the bottom of an ever-increasing council house waiting list. For them the only bathroom they were likely to encounter for years ahead was on a local cinema screen.

It is therefore not surprising that so many remember the long-vanished bath night procedure, often with great amusement, beginning with the tin bath being taken down from its hook on the outside brewhouse wall and dragged indoors to be placed on the hearth in front of a roaring fire. Many slum dwellings had no indoor water supply so there followed the ritual of heaving kettles and jugs of water from the outside tap before placing them on the fireside hob to heat.

Depending on how many of the family were taking a bath, it would entail a continuous process of refilling the bath. For large families in a household of both boys and girls, there was the added embarrassing problem of stopping anyone entering the room while someone of the opposite sex was in the bath. Occasionally the odd mishap would occur but when this happened, after a brief argument, bath night would continue as normal.

It was an era when girls in particular were expected to do a proportion of weekly domestic jobs without complaining. Such duties included helping with dusting and general cleaning, making beds, ironing and shopping. For most hard-pressed housewives the evenings would bring an opportunity to take a short respite from their domestic routine, but it never lasted long.

There was always the usual batch of mending and darning to be done and on dark winter nights, old clothes would be cut up for rug-making using a tool called a bodger and a hessian sack. Any other spare time would be utilised for knitting garments for the whole family and, finally, before retiring to bed, sandwiches would be prepared for working members of the household to take to work next morning.

Getting a bargain

Weekends meant little respite from the drudgery of household duties. There was, for instance, the usual Saturday late night jaunt to market looking for cheap purchases, which always coincided with stallholders desperately seeking to dispose of any perishable food items prior to closing time.

Most municipal markets stayed open until 9 p.m. on a Saturday, and with limited refrigeration, the only way traders could avoid a total loss on anything perishable was by tempting people with give-away bargains – otherwise it would be dumped. Shrewd Black Country housewives were fully aware of this weekly late-night situation and were content to hang around to obtain the best value for every penny they spent.

Quite often it was possible to purchase a whole rabbit with a leg of pork thrown in for sixpence and all kinds of fruit and confectionery were sold at practically give-away prices.

Every Sunday was regarded as the ideal opportunity to visit relatives and was a welcomed break from household tasks for a brief time. The occasion would be

Old Wednesbury Market, where a bargain could be secured on a Saturday night. (Reproduced by permission of Sandwell Community History and Archive Service)

used to exchange news of the past week's family activities and catching up on various events.

Without the aid of any domestic electrical gadgets and the modern-day cleansing products, maintaining the family home was always a repetitive and physically challenging task for any woman during the early part of the twentieth century.

Each day of the week housewives used their considerable household skills and wit to feed and clothe the family, while keeping the home clean and tidy, mostly on a pittance of a weekly budget.

Household rules of discipline and punishment

Whenever senior citizens talk about family rules that applied throughout their childhood, they inevitably refer to that old adage 'Children should be seen and not heard.' This philosophy was instigated religiously at home and in public with youngsters expected to keep a low profile during the entire period of their juvenile years.

A group of children from the Horsley Fields area of Wolverhampton, 1930s.

This meant knowing their place at all times and understanding they should never ask questions that might prove to be embarrassing or awkward for their parents to answer. In similar fashion they were discouraged from ever eavesdropping on adult conversations.

If they did listen in and then query what they had overheard, it usually resulted in a parent responding with the familiar proverb, 'little pigs have big ears.' A rebuke sufficient to deter any further questioning. Such a response would also be used whenever a child decided to play up with a display of tantrums. In most instances, a swift word of restraint accompanied by an angry parental stare would usually be enough to end the errant behaviour.

At times, a parent would also administer a sharp clip around the ear, or if appropriate, a mild smack across the legs. In some families, for exceptional bad behaviour, boys would be threatened with the father's strap.

One type of misdemeanour that would never be treated lightly was that of being a nuisance to neighbours. An unwritten code of conduct existed that every youngster should respect all adults, especially those who happened to live in the same street or courtyard. If a neighbour found it necessary to complain to a mother about her offspring's unreasonable behaviour, the child involved would be immediately confronted with the dreaded words 'I shall tell your father when he gets home, so just get your bones ready.' This would be enough to bring forth belated cries of immediate repentance, because in those days, the prospect of trying to explain any such misdemeanour to a stern father was a situation to be avoided at all costs.

As part of the normal process of growing up in a pre-war community, children quickly learned that doing anything that conflicted with their parents' strict rules of conduct was very unwise. A much-favoured method of discipline used for minor offences involved sending a child to bed early. This would mean missing out on the opportunity of staying up late to enjoy playing games with friends until well past the usual bedtime deadline, especially on a beautiful summer evening.

At meal times, any child deciding to become finicky with the food placed before them would soon be told to 'either eat it or do without and go hungry,' and usually this had the desired effect. Another firm rule was that under no circumstances should a child talk back to an adult or complain about the inadequacy of their weekly pocket money. Likewise they would also never attempt to criticise the types of clothes or shoes provided for them as such disrespect would simply not be tolerated.

In the home, every youngster would be expected to obey their parents' command immediately and without dissent and swearing in any shape or form was strictly forbidden.

Between the 1930s and '50s, the majority of children were part of a large extended family unit living within close proximity to each other, and there was always an obligatory duty imposed on children to visit their grandparents and various uncles and aunts at least once a week, mainly on a Sunday morning. Many people remember this as being an irksome family duty because such jaunts required youngsters to make strenuous efforts to ensure they kept their precious Sunday best clothes spotlessly clean throughout their stay.

On arrival, they knew only to well that they would be expected to sit quietly and not fidget while being forced to listen to endless adult chatter about tedious, boring grown-up matters. They were expected to speak only when spoken to, make little noise, never spill drinks on the floor or drop crumbs on the front room carpet, and because it was the Sabbath day, they were forbidden to participate in any type of ball game.

When looking back, most people maintain that such discipline was, in the main, fair and just, and such rules helped to keep youngsters on the right path. Most are convinced that the minor forms of corporal punishment administered by their parents did them more good than harm.

Running errands

It was once an accepted part of family life that when a child reached a certain age they would be considered capable of running errands. One of the most commonplace involved being despatched to the local coal merchants to collect the essential supply of coal. This would be carefully weighed on the scales before being taken away in a heavy wheelbarrow loaned from the yard. Usually it was a hundredweight load, which would be pushed along the street and upon reaching home, quickly tipped down an open cellar entrance located at the front of the house.

In properties without this facility, it was customary to place the contents in a corner of the outside brewhouse and then the borrowed barrow would be returned to the coal yard. For those living in a house that relied solely on old-style smelly oil lamps for lighting, the most important task was visiting the nearest lamp-oil supplier to purchase the necessary quantity required to keep the lamps alight. This, too, was an errand allocated to youngsters.

Once a child was considered old enough they would also be expected to undertake the chore of going to the local shops to purchase perishable items of food which, due to the scarcity of suitable cool storage space in most dwellings, made it vital to buy on a daily basis.

Many of the older generation have sharp memories of being given precise instructions about shopping correctly, which were firmly drummed into them prior to leaving the house. Children would be sent to the bakers, butchers, greengrocers, and on Fridays, to the local fish and chip shop – especially in a Catholic household, because it was a fasting day with no meat allowed.

In addition to all the clear instructions about doing the shopping properly, the children would always be given the obligatory small piece of paper containing a list of the items with the individual price marked alongside and the amount of change the child was expected to bring back.

Every youngster dreaded the thought of arriving home with less than the amount of change indicated on the shopping list, because they were fully aware that they would be sent back to the shop to ask the shopkeeper to explain why certain items had increased in price.

Although such a situation was guaranteed to make youngsters feel acutely embarrassed, most understood only to well that their mother needed to make sure every single penny of family income was spent wisely, which is why the vast majority of today's housewives from that era became very astute in the domestic art of identifying and only buying the best value brands available.

One typical example from that era is that of a Darlaston housewife who could neither read or write, but always knew the best food prices on offer from day to day to the extent that no local corner shop would ever attempt to overcharge her or even try to fob her off with a more expensive product.

People who grew up with the custom of children taking responsibility for running errands as a normal part of their lives are adamant the experience provided a good grounding for adulthood. For girls especially, regular shopping expeditions taught them how to manage a home on a low income, and the ways and means of spotting the best bargains. A minority of youngsters would go a stage further by volunteering to carry out errands for their neighbours, particularly as it usually resulted in being given a small reward to spend on sweets or a comic.

In most Black Country households strict ground rules were applied relating to any financial inducements for doing any errand. Most children received a fixed weekly amount of pocket money, and any reward for going on any errand would usually relate to that level. Other than that, any additional spending money had to be earned by taking a part-time job, such as a paper round, delivering groceries, or helping out in a local shop. Even after leaving school many girls opted to do part-time work as an usherette in a cinema or theatre, mainly to obtain the clothes or shoes that their parents could not afford to buy for them. Consequently, throughout the 1930s, '40s and '50s at the beginning of their working life, young people were prepared to do this extra work to give them a certain amount of financial independence.

Advice on the best methods of raising children

In the Black Country, the traditional extended family unit consisted of grandparents, uncles and aunts, together with numerous first and second cousins. Many lived close to each other in back street properties, or communal courtyards, resulting in a strong bond of caring for each others' welfare, and this was particularly so in relation to the overall welfare of children.

This type of inter-family involvement was inevitable because they crossed each other's paths virtually everyday. It is therefore not surprising that older members of a family regularly became involved in keeping a watchful eye on youngsters. Every child was well aware that if they were seen misbehaving by a close relative in public, they would be admonished on the spot. Worse still, their actions would almost certainly be reported back to their parents.

A typical close-knit Black Country family group of the 1930s.

Older, more experienced relatives, such as grandparents, parents, uncles or aunts would offer suggestions and advice on certain matters to young married couples relating to problems of raising children. This was always the case when illness struck such as measles, chicken pox, croup, tuberculosis or the dreaded diphtheria. Any helpful counselling would be welcomed, especially during the decades prior to the modern health service when few could afford a doctor.

Even when children left school and started to work some matriarchal grandmothers expected to be consulted regularly by sons and daughters and kept informed on how the respective grandchildren were progressing. This offering of advice and direct interference with the methods of raising children would undoubtedly be totally rejected by today's parents.

The children's role in looking after their parents in their old age

The once-accepted tradition of sons and daughters bearing ultimate responsibility for parents in their twilight years is now no longer commonplace. On the contrary, such an attitude is now regarded as being totally outdated. In the early years of the twentieth century, whenever a parent died it was the tradition, especially in a large family, for one of the married children to offer accommodation in their home to the surviving father or mother, rather than see them spend their remaining years living on their own. This solution would be arrived at following discussions involving the whole family, and always included a commitment for the other sons and daughters to promise to give their support, and share the responsibility in any way possible.

Prior to the early 1960s there was a massive scarcity of purpose-built dwellings for the elderly in the Black Country. This also applied to direct local council social service provision. Older people were furiously independent and many preferred to live out their twilight years in the same house where they had raised their families but inevitably the size of the property, cost of heating and repairs made things very difficult.

For those fortunate to have a married son or daughter living in the same neighbourhood, such shortcomings were hardly a problem because ready help was always nearby, to take on the responsibilities of gardening, shopping, washing, or, when needed, cooking. Nowadays, families tend to live many miles away from each other and that type of support is not available when most needed. Added to this is the fact that the custom of children accepting an obligation for the welfare of ageing parents no longer exists. Modern society seems to believe that the vast present-day social welfare system will attend adequately to the individual requirements and circumstances of senior citizens.

Unfortunately, time and time again, the true realities prove this to be completely the opposite.

The older generation claim there are important lessons to be learned from looking back at the way communities once coped with the massive challenge of caring for the old and infirm at a time of virtually no state assistance or welfare benefits.

With an ever-increasing ageing population, radical changes would have to be made in overall attitudes to pensioners, by perhaps adopting some of those solutions followed by previous generations towards this ever-present problem of looking after the most vulnerable in society.

CHAPTER ELEVEN

Entertainment

How the wireless changed traditional family lifestyles

The established order of family life underwent a major upheaval in the 1920s and '30s due to the rapid expansion of wireless broadcasting. It revolutionised the way people entertained themselves and changed many aspects of normal social behaviour. One example in the Black Country was the decline in the popular practice of groups of people assembling on a Sunday evening in someone's front room, often following attendance at evening services, for a chat over sandwiches, a glass of beer or tea and then commencing a customary sing-along session around the piano.

Increased broadcasting hours also gradually brought about a marked falling away in the pastime of reading for leisure. From the mid-1920s the number of wireless sets in the country leaped from a few thousand to over three million and everyone was quite happy to take out the required licence at a cost of 10*s*.

In those pioneering years, sets were powered by ugly, awkward accumulators fitted with a wooden handle for carrying purposes, but the power they provided was strictly limited, making it necessary to regularly visit the nearest local dealer for the accumulator to be recharged for a small fee. There are many who still remember making these frequent treks to the local wireless shop. It was a chore no member of the family welcomed with any enthusiasm because on the homeward journey, during the process of trying to keep the accumulator upright, it would inevitably tilt slightly at some point, resulting in a tiny quantity of acid overflow spilling over the hand. This caused a sharp burning sensation that was very irritating.

This is why everyone welcomed the first appearance of all-electric valve sets, which rendered the cumbersome accumulator obsolete virtually overnight. Most of these new models were fashionably encased in the new style bakelite material, which was to become very popular in the early 1930s. Soon it began to be used by manufacturers on an assortment of everyday household items.

People vividly remember those early broadcasting years when the wireless slowly became an indispensable part of daily lifestyles; a period now looked back on as the first genuine wireless era. Over the 1930s and '40s, a clear policy of broadcasting standards was instituted within a specific code of practice. This covered guidelines on bad language, defamation, sexual innuendo, and above all, every type of political or religious comment. Throughout that period the BBC retained a complete monopoly of the airwaves apart from the lightweight presence of two very small commercial stations, Radio Luxemburg and Radio Normandy, both of which provided limited hours of transmission offering a mixture of recorded music, quiz shows and children's programmes.

Among the best remembered personalities were the likes of Tommy Handley, Gracie Fields, Jack Warner, Arthur Askey, Richard Murdoch, Rob Wilton, Elsie and Doris Waters, Sandy Powell, Donald Peers and Max Miller to name but a few.

Dance band broadcasts and ballroom dancing

Initially, from the early 1930s, a standard electric-powered wireless cost around £12 and as sales continued to increase, an expansion of daily programmes began that attracted huge listening figures. The BBC introduced regular dance band broadcasts and in 1933 achieved a technical breakthrough with the first ever live outdoor transmissions direct from top London hotels such as the Savoy, Dorchester, and Mayfair bringing the unique sounds of famous orchestras into millions of homes. Those live shows became immensely popular and also created a new interest in all types of ballroom dancing. Private and municipal dance venues all over the Black Country region benefited from large crowds eager to try out the latest dance routines.

Included among the best-remembered dance bands of those halcyon broadcasting days were Ambrose, Geraldo, Billy Cotton, Roy Fox, Henry Hall, Jack Payne, Joe Loss and Harry Roy. Each extended their fame through the BBC's daily transmissions as did their resident singers, stars like Ann Shelton, Al Bowlly, Vera Lynn, Denny Dennis, Donald Peers and many others. Later, in addition to the output of live outside night-time ballroom music, similar lunchtime and teatime live big band broadcasting were introduced which further added to the enormous interest in ballroom dancing.

When any of the famous bands went on tour it resulted in a total sell-out of tickets as numerous local newspaper reports and photographs of eager fans dancing or just listening to their favourite orchestras and singers clearly confirm. Around the same time, a significant technical advance in the system of gramophone production swept the country. Previously, the only type of

Jack Andrews' local dance band, 1940s/'50s.

gramophone available in shops was the old-fashioned cumbersome wind-up model. Elderly people recall that these portable contraptions were clumsy and operated by vigorously turning a winding handle fixed to the side. This ensured the turntable continued to move at the required speed. In addition a steel-playing needle had to be screwed into a round-shaped headpiece mounted on the end of the playing arm extension, which was then placed on the record for playing. After a while the continuous pressure would create scratches on the record's surface interfering with the sound quality and making damaging scratch marks.

The new technological innovation changed all that in the shape of an electric-driven motor complete with a lightweight turntable that allowed a stack of up to six records to be played in one session. The light pick-up arm extension moved across each record with hardly any pressure, eliminating possible surface damage and providing high quality reproduction.

Originally this technical breakthrough was confined to radiograms – a very advanced combined radio and gramophone unit encased in a smart wooden veneer cabinet usually found in only the best homes, because of their initial high

Ballroom dancing became incredibly popular in the Black Country.

costs. Possessing one became the new status symbol, taking the place of the once-prized piano of previous decades.

From about 1925, the wireless had become part of people's daily lives and in 1926 during the General Strike it was the only regular source of public information because of the absence of daily newspapers. However, it was to be the mid-1930s when it reached its highest level of popularity.

The BBC meets the demands of a younger audience

The BBC regularly claimed that it always tried to satisfy every part of its vast audience. Many would refute that fact by pointing out that until the late 1940s there was a lack of programmes likely to appeal to teenagers. This continued into the early post-war years when the commercial stations such as Radio Luxemburg began broadcasts featuring famous recording artists of the day, mainly aimed directly at younger listeners.

A new Sunday night programme called *Top Twenty* began to attract a massive following of that age group. Even though it was transmitted at the late hours of 11 to 12 p.m., it very quickly became the first cult radio chart show. The reason for its success was the number of records sold in record shops because the programme producers gambled that a top twenty list would stimulate the interest of the younger members of the public. This led to a swift upsurge in record sales. People tuned in to try to predict the position of their favourite record each week.

This was undoubtedly the forerunner of all subsequent pop chart programmes and it became a Sunday night must for thousands of young men doing their National Service. Many from the Black Country fondly recall sitting around a primitive stove in their barracks listening to *Top Twenty* and trying to guess the week's number one record.

In response to this challenge, the BBC initiated a series of their own record shows, for example, *Two Way Family Favourites*, *The Jack Jackson Record Show*, *Forces Favourites* and a special weekday morning record request programme called *Housewives' Choice*. Finally they introduced solely for children a programme broadcast on Saturday morning called *Children's Choice*.

During 1952, a sensational new recording technical breakthrough occurred with the appearance of the long-playing record that not only provided longer recordings but its sapphire playing needle provided the sharpest quality record reproduction yet heard. This was the time when practically every household possessed one of the unforgettable family treasures of the 1950s, a portable Dansette record player. They became familiar in most homes as young and old built up their collection of new style long-playing records.

American orchestras become immensely popular from the early 1940s

In the late 1940s and early '50s American dance bands and singers were very popular and people still enjoy reminiscing about them because of the impact they had on their social lives. Among the most treasured memories are those of Tommy Dorsey, Benny Goodman, Artie Shaw, Woody Herman, Harry James and most of all the unique Glenn Miller Orchestra.

Also revered were recording artists Bing Crosby, Judy Garland, Ella Fitzgerald, June Allyson, Alice Faye, Peggy Lee, Jo Stafford, Doris Day, Dick Haymes, Perry Como and the legendary Frank Sinatra. Their distinctive sound would echo throughout the Black Country in dance halls, youth clubs and music shops and every town council promoted weekly hops in either their municipal hall or public baths that included music with an American influence.

They proved such an attraction that some local authorities organised inter-town dancing contests to provide added interest, but the thing most people recollect are just how tame those events were. Anyone even slightly misbehaving would be ejected and at the many popular organised church dances held in the local community halls, there was never any likelihood of alcohol abuse because the only drinks available would be ginger beer, orange or perhaps a light shandy.

It was a period when the region contained numerous dancing schools with qualified instructors providing weekly courses for a moderate fee. Thousands of real ballroom dancing zealots would also avidly tune in to the Victor Sylvester dance instruction programme on the wireless, with a selected dance step given to listeners to be followed from a diagram inserted in the *Radio Times*, which most Black Country households purchased every week.

Christmas

The festive season was always eagerly anticipated and even in the pre-war period of limited public holidays, the meagre normally two days' break was something to look forward to. It provided the ideal occasion for organising a family party, but it was also an opportunity to observe the religious aspect of the festive season. Usually much of the serious preparations would have started in mid-November, but for those struggling on a very low income, the preparations would have to began much earlier, because of the necessary financial restrictions.

Almost certainly most parents had for months made financial sacrifices by contributing to a local Christmas Club Fund to ensure particular toys could be purchased for their children. For countless households this was the only way the added expense could be met, and in that era the majority of young children generally acknowledged the fact that their parents had little spare money for luxury items and, therefore, were always grateful for whatever presents they received.

To obtain some seasonal extra money to buy small gifts for their parents and friends, many youngsters went carol singing during the final week prior to the big day. Unlike the modern day version of this traditional custom, it would be carefully organised to avoid any possible unwarranted intrusion outside people's homes, which meant that most adults had no objection and were prepared to offer a small contribution. Some enterprising children were even more adventurous having the foresight to seek the permission of local landlords to make a brief call at their public houses to sing a carol or two which guaranteed a useful financial return.

With so many families living in close proximity to each other, Christmas parties became the social highlight of the year, with weeks of discussions and suggestions about catering and sleeping arrangements for members of the family attending from longer distances.

Inevitably the celebrations would go on into the early hours of Boxing Day with singing around the piano. Individual people insisted on performing their once-a-year party piece, and there would be dancing, fancy dress, very often concluding with a noisy version of the popular conga dance routine flowing on to the street and back. All of these activities would be maintained with a liberal supply of drink and the continuous supply of all types of sandwiches, with everyone determined to enjoy every minute knowing full well that it would be another twelve months before another similar family get-together could be repeated.

After Christmas and Boxing Day, people would have to wait until Easter Monday for another break, because even 1 January was a full working day until 1974, when it became an additional public holiday.

During the weeks running up to the festive period, children would help to make paper decorations and spend some of their pocket money on buying small ornaments to place on the traditional tree. Few Christmas puddings were bought from a shop; most would be made at home months before. The vast majority of greeting cards were sent through the post, with the cost being relatively low, unlike the present day with the ever-rising cost of a stamps.

Few working class families could afford crackers because even then the average price of a normal box was £1 5*s*, which made them far too expensive and until the early 1950s most domestic seasonal trees were lit up with colourful wax candles.

Before shops and stores adopted the awful modern practice of starting the countdown to Christmas in early September, most children happily anticipated the traditional visit to one of their local grotto displays with great excitement. The opportunity to gaze in awe at the wide selection of toys was worth waiting for, plus the added thrill of meeting Santa and receiving a small gift. Sadly, with all the prolonged weeks of blatant commercialisation of today, the experience has almost entirely lost its magic.

From the mid-1950s, prolonged television adverts have become a dominant feature of the festive season. Intensive advertising was designed to encourage young people to pressurise their parents into purchasing the latest designer clothes, popular toy or electrical gadget no matter what the cost.

Older people fondly recall that in their youth, toys were uncomplicated and fairly cheap in relation to the average family income. For both boys and girls it usually meant a mixture of the popular compendium of games, selection box of chocolates, the obligatory adventure book, or comic annual and various magazines. Top of the wanted list of presents for girls would be either a doll and pram, black board and easel, nurses uniform, spinning top, or a three-wheeled bicycle, and for boys a clockwork train, dart board, wooden fort with soldiers, dinky car model, aeroplane, pedal car, cowboy outfit or possibly a Meccano construction set. Every child's stocking would be supplemented with an apple, orange and a selection of nuts, drawing books and pencils and possibly a box of paints, and perhaps a jigsaw.

One other old custom that is now becoming rarer and rarer is the tradition of Christmas dinner at home with the family. There are two main reasons for this trend. One is the tendency for families to become scattered all over the country and the other is the rapid rise in popularity of public house catering, which along with extensive television viewing, and a much longer holiday break is drastically changing the way the festive period is celebrated throughout the region.

The other casualty of deliberate commercialisation of the season is, of course, the declining religious factor which once saw entire families either attending midnight services or early daytime celebrations, with people happily exchanging greetings after each service before hurrying home for that first obligatory Christmas drink.

A further image of that has disappeared over the years is the traditional football games that always took place on Christmas morning, when housewives were only too glad to see the men get out from under their feet and go off to a match. Older men reminiscence about the familiar sight and smell of the cigars they received as Christmas present and the way the unique aroma would sweep across the terraces, bringing back happy memories of bygone days. Others would take a quick swig from the rum or whisky in their flasks given to them as presents to keep out the cold.

The idea of modern-day pampered soccer players having to play on such a day is now unthinkable, as is the vision of smoking cigars and dipping into a warming flask. Under the present-day restrictive laws on drink driving, and smoking they are now only memories of the region's past and part of life as it once was.

CHAPTER TWELVE

Heritage

During the once-powerful industrial past of the Black Country region, the local workforce could make whatever goods or merchandise the trading world required, and if an item wasn't immediately available, ways and means would soon be devised of manufacturing it to meet the demand. The fact that this proud boast that almost anything could be made in the area no longer applies is a matter of great sadness to older residents. They also deplore how they had to witness, throughout the 1970s and '80s, the closure

John Harper foundry, Willenhall.

of so many local companies. Household names such as Revo, Guy Motors, Patent Shaft, Sankeys, Bigwoods, Rubery Owen, Henry Meadows, Round Oak Steel Works, Ever Ready, GKN Sankeys, Thompson Brothers, Charles Richards, Stewart & Lloyds, John Harper and British Heat Resisting Glass Company (Phoenix Glass) have all disappeared, to name but a few.

The goods and materials they produced, established the worldwide reputation of the region for reliability and the special skills of its workforce. The collapse of so many industries over such a short stretch of time has been a social disaster accelerating the end of traditional Black Country communities. Incredibly this once-thriving centre of industrial enterprise and trade skills has since become a manufacturing wasteland. People have also had to come to terms with the fact that the industrial legacy created by the skills, hard work and dedication of their grandparents and parents which they believed would flourish and provide employment for many later generation is now but a shattered illusion.

They now feel that the industrial legacy created by previous generations, through their hard work and dedication, has been destroyed and the region is fast becoming nothing more than a collection of uniform dormitory towns made up of endless DIY stores, charity shops, banks, office blocks, supermarkets, leisure centres, take-aways, along with site after site of small engineering firms employing only a handful of people. Future historians will find it difficult to explain how this area of immense industrial power was allowed to simply wither away well before the end of the twentieth century.

Summary

Thank you for taking the time to read this book, which hopefully you found interesting and informative. Apart from the inclusion of certain necessary dates, facts and figures associated with particular historic events, every detail has been contributed by ordinary local men and women. Many are sadly no longer with us, but from the outset they willingly provided access to their personal experiences with the clear understanding that part of any proceeds would be given to a worthwhile charity.

From these priceless recollections it is clearly evident that people's day-to-day lives were very similar in many respects, and consequently they have been amalgamated to give a consistent portrait of daily working class life in that era. As an example, working conditions and wages for anyone employed in a foundry for instance in Darlaston turned out to be almost identical to those of someone working in a foundry located in Wednesbury, Bilston, Willenhall or any other local town.

This was also applicable to the overall quality of people's lives, be it poor housing, low standards of health care, lack of recreational facilities, ridiculously low weekly incomes, and as a direct consequence a very restrictive social life. Such circumstances would prevail in the majority of households throughout the first fifty years of the century and undoubtedly events and living conditions over those decades became important defining moments in the ups and downs of the region's history.

For Black Country people, the years since the beginning of the twentieth century was a period of great transformation, depression, tragedy and change, but in spite of this, the true spirit of the region lives on.